B

L. SHAKESPEARE, WILLIAM

DATE

2

Presented
to

THE ANGLICAN COMMUNITY

SCHOOL OF ST. MARK

BY

THE BRIDGER FAMILY

1988

SHAKESPEARE

SHAKESPEARE

Christopher Martin

Life and Works

Jane Austen
The Brontës
Thomas Hardy
Ernest Hemingway
D. H. Lawrence
Katherine Mansfield
George Orwell
Shakespeare
H. G. Wells
Virginia Woolf

Cover illustration by David Armitage

First published in 1988 by
Wayland (Publishers) Ltd
61 Western Road, Hove,
East Sussex BN3 1JD, England

Series adviser: Dr Cornelia Cook
Series designer: David Armitage
Editor: Sophie Davies

British Library Cataloguing in Publication Data

Martin, Christopher
    Shakespeare—(Life and works)
    1. Shakespeare, William—Study and teaching
    I. Title
    822.3'3   PR 2987

ISBN 1-85210-418-X

Typeset, printed and bound in the UK
by The Bath Press, Avon

Contents

1 The Mystery of Shakespeare

Thomas Hardy's memorial poem, 'To Shakespeare after 300 years', written in 1916, imagines the playwright dying in Stratford-upon-Avon 300 years before. The citizens of the town, hearing the funeral bell toll for him, might not, Hardy considers, have been deeply disturbed; after all, his working life had been spent in London and they did not know him well:

I'faith, few knew him much here, save by word,
He having elsewhere led his busier life;
Though to be sure he left with us his wife.'
– Ah, one of the tradesmen's sons, I now recall . . .
   Witty, I've heard . . .
We did not know him . . . Well, good-day. Death comes to all.'

Just as, Hardy continues, the Stratford people respected Shakespeare's success but knew little of him personally, so we, modern readers and theatre-goers, admire Shakespeare's works but know almost nothing about him as a human being. There is the strange contrast of the huge, world-wide fame and the relative obscurity of the man. It is little wonder, then, that in the same poem Hardy saw him as a mystery, a 'bright baffling soul'.

Why is there this mystery surrounding Shakespeare, especially when the lives of other Elizabethans and Jacobeans are relatively well known? Although Shakespeare did much to advance the status of his craft, actors were not highly regarded in his time, and theatres were often

Opposite *The seventeenth century Chandos portrait may be authentic. With its famous earring, it is perhaps the most attractive of the many portraits of Shakespeare.*

6

IVDICIO PYLIVM GENIO SOCRATEM ARTE MARONEM,
TERRA TEGIT, POPVLVS MÆRET, OLYMPVS HABET

STAY PASSENGER, WHY GOEST THOV BY SO FAST,
READ IF THOV CANST, WHOM ENVIOVS DEATH HATH PLAST
WITH IN THIS MONVMENT SHAKSPEARE: WITH WHOME,
QVICK NATVRE DIDE WHOSE NAME, DOTH DECK Y. TOMBE,
FAR MORE, THEN COST: SIEH ALL, Y. HE HATH WRITT,
LEAVES LIVING ART, BVT PAGE, TO SERVE HIS WITT.

considered to be dangerous social nuisances. Sir Thomas Bodley did not even want to collect 'idle books and riff-raff ... such as plays' for his Oxford Library, opened in 1612. In this climate, therefore, Shakespeare, and those who knew him, could not have imagined that he would become so important and famous in the future. Shakespeare perhaps thought of his investments and property as his most durable achievement: he, wrote the poet Alexander Pope,

> For gain not glory, winged his roving flight
> And grew immortal in his own despite.

So it was that his conversation was not recorded, his letters not kept, his library dispersed, even his precious play manuscripts lost.

What, then, is left to record his life and character? Of several portraits, only two are trustworthy: the memorial bust in Holy Trinity Church, Stratford, approved by his family, and the Droeshout engraving that appears in the First Folio edition of the plays: Ben Jonson said this was a likeness, wishing the engraver could have 'drawn his wit/As well in brass, as he hath hit his face ...' Of the others, the Chandos portrait, with the earring, is the most human and attractive.

There are a few scraps of handwriting: the several signatures which are certainly Shakespeare's, and three pages of manuscript from a play of uncertain date, *Sir Thomas More*, which he may have composed with other dramatists.

There are scattered comments by people who actually knew him: his fellow actors and first editors, John Heminges and Henry Condell, for example, or his rival playwright, Ben Jonson, who left a few notes.

I loved the man and do honour his memory (on this side idolatry) as much as any. He was indeed honest, and of an open and free nature; had an excellent fancy [imagination], brave notions and gentle expressions; wherein he flowed with that facility, that sometimes it was necessary he should be stopped.

(Ben Jonson, *Discoveries*, 1637)

Shakespeare memorabilia, dating from the late seven-

Opposite The memorial bust, ordered by Shakespeare's family from a stonemason's near the Globe Theatre in London, is probably an accurate portrait. It stands near Shakespeare's grave in Holy Trinity Church, Stratford

9

Martin Droeshout sculpsit London.

To the Reader.

This *Figure*, that thou here seest put,
   It was for gentle *Shakespeare* cut
Wherein the *Graver* had a strife
   With *Nature*, to out-doe the *Life* :
O, could he but have drawn his *Wit*
   As well in *Brasse*, as he has hit
His *Face* ; the *Print* would then surpasse
   All, that was ever writ in *Brasse*.
But since he cannot, *Reader*, look
   Not on his *Picture*, but his *Book*.

                         B. I.

teenth or eighteenth centuries, are an unreliable source. They tell us that he poached deer in Charlecote Park, near Stratford, that his first London job was holding gentlemen's horses outside theatres, and so on. There may be seeds of truth in these stories, as their collectors, such as John Aubrey, spoke to people who had known the great writer. Certainly these anecdotes add colour to the life story.

There are the million words of the plays and poems. George Bernard Shaw, the modern playwright, claimed that 'With the plays and sonnets in our hands, we know more about Shakespeare than we know about Dickens'. The works certainly tell us something about Shakespeare's reading, but their ideas and characters are so varied that almost anything could be proved from them.

Finally there are the official documentary records – baptisms, burials, marriage papers, property purchases, legal cases and tax records. One of these – a London law case of 1612, in which Shakespeare gave some rather vague evidence – is the only record we have of his actual words on any subject. However, on the whole this source reveals little of the playwright as a man.

Frustration with these records has led in two directions. Eighteenth-century researchers were sure there must be more and better material. They were haunted by the idea of 'two chests', supposedly crammed with Shakespearean papers and manuscripts. A lawyer's clerk, William Ireland, claimed to trace these to Clopton Manor, near Stratford, where the owner told him he had recently destroyed 'several basketsfull of letters and papers . . . and as to Shakespeare, there were many bundles with his name wrote upon them . . . In this very fireplace I made a roaring bonfire of them.' Thus disappointed, Ireland set about forging Shakespeare material: a letter to Anne Hathaway, the manuscript of *King Lear*, and a lost play, *Vortigern*, which was performed once in London before it was exposed as a fraud.

Disappointment with the apparent ordinariness of the man revealed by research also led to the early twentieth-century theories of the 'Anti-Stratfordians'. Convinced that the plays could not have been written by a man from such a humble background, these eccentric writers suggested they were the disguised work of other men: Francis Bacon, Christopher Marlowe (who did not, they

11

[Secretary hand manuscript — the "Hand D" addition to the play Sir Thomas More (British Library Harley MS 7368, folio 9a)]

9

   moor   Nay Certainly you ar

for to the king god hath his offyce lent
of dread of Iustyce, power and Comaund
hath bid him rule, and willd yow to obay
and to add ampler maieste to this
he hath not only lent the king his figure
his throne & sword, but gyven him his owne name
calls him a god on earth, what do yow then
rysing gainst him that god himsealf enstalls
but ryse gainst god, what do yow to yo{u}r sowles
in doing this o desperat as you are.
wash your foule mynds wt teares and those same hands
that yow lyke rebells lyft against the peace
lyft vp for peace, and your vnreuerent knees
make them your feet to kneele to be forgyven

tell me but this, what rebell captaine
as mutynes ar incident, by his name
can still the rout who will obay a traytor
or howe can well that proclamation sounde
when ther is no adicion but a rebell
to quallyfy a rebell, youle put downe straingers
kyll them cutt their throts possesse their howses
and leade the matie of lawe in liom
to slipp him lyke a hound ; saye nowe the king
as he is clement, yf thoffendor moorne
shoold so much com to short of your great trespas
as but to banish yow, whether woold yow go.
what Country by the nature of your error
shoold gyve yow harber go yow to ffraunc or flanders
to any Iarman p{ro}vince, spane or portigall
nay any where that not adheres to Ingland
why yow must needs be straingers, woold yow be pleasd
to find a nation of such barbarous temper
that breaking out in hiddious violence
woold not afford yow, an abode on earth
whett their detested knyves against your throts
spurne yow lyke doggs, and lyke as yf that god
owed not nor made not yow, nor that the elaments
wer not all appropriat to yo{u}r Comforts.
but Charterd vnto them, what would yow thinck
to be thus vsd, this is the straingers case
and this your mountanish inhumanyty

   all   faith a saies trewe, letts do as we may be doon by

   Linco   weele be ruld by yow master moor yf youle stand our ...

said, die in 1593 but wrote on from secret exile in Italy), the Earls of Oxford or Derby, even Queen Elizabeth herself! Clues were supposedly found in the plays: for example, the long Latin word *honorificabilitudinitatibus* in *Love's Labours Lost* is claimed to be an anagram for other Latin words meaning 'These plays, the offspring of Francis Bacon, are preserved for the world'. The 'Anti-Stratfordians' are now largely discredited: we can easily accept that, by the chances of heredity, a great genius may appear from any social background.

Fresh material still appears, and there must surely be more to discover. In 1985, a poem 'Shall I die?' credited with Shakepeare's name, was 're-discovered' in the Bodleian Library, Oxford. Here is one verse from it:

> In a dream it did seem –
> But alas, dreams do pass
>   as do shadows –
> I did walk, I did talk
> With my love, with my dove,
>   through fair meadows.
> Still we passed till at last
> We sat to repose us for pleasure.
> Being set, lips met
> Arms twined, and did bind my heart's treasure.

(Bodleian Library MS, c. 1593–5)

Though we have many facts to give us an outline of Shakespeare's career, what we lack is something more personal that would clear the fog that surrounds Shakespeare and show us something of the human being beyond the documented facts.

Opposite Some scholars believe that this page from Sir Thomas More, *a play composed by several writers, is in Shakespeare's handwriting. Certain lines have been crossed out by the Court censor.*

Shakespeare's signature: a few examples survive on various documents.

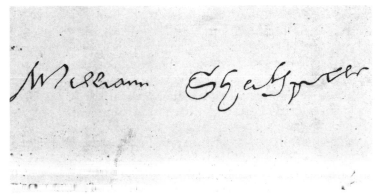

13

2 Youth in Stratford-upon-Avon

Whatever his triumphs in London, Shakespeare's birthplace, Stratford-upon-Avon in Warwickshire, remained the true centre of his life.

Sixteenth-century Stratford was a proud, thriving community of 1,500 to 2,000 people. Its several important annual markets attracted goods and craftsmen from miles around. With its grid of broad streets, lined with half-timbered houses, inns and shops, its many orchards, its thousand elm trees, it was justly described in William Camden's *Britannia* (1586) as 'handsome'.

Stratford was surrounded by rich farmland, still cultivated by the strip system of Medieval times. In the mid-sixteenth century, at Wilmcote, three miles north-west of the town, lived Robert Arden, a gentleman farmer related to a distinguished Warwickshire family. His estate at Snitterfield was farmed by his tenant, Richard Shakespeare, William's grandfather. One of his sons, John, was ambitious and moved into Stratford to seek his fortune in business.

He chose the glove trade, a profitable one as manufacturers were protected by Parliament against foreign competition. It was also a powerful trade in the town, with its stalls placed centrally by the clock tower in the market square. Technically John Shakespeare was a 'whittawer', who prepared and sold the best light-coloured leather, although, like other Stratford traders, he probably dealt in other commodities, such as timber, barley or wool. John became rich enough to purchase the western half

of the house where he lodged in Henley Street (now famous as William's birthplace), eventually buying the other half and more property besides. Meanwhile he began to rise through the hierarchy of wealthy tradesmen who ruled the town's affairs, beginning in 1556 as 'ale taster', one who controlled the price and quality of basic foodstuffs. Five years later he moved on to the Council as one of the fourteen burgesses.

Above *Shakespeare was probably born in his father's house in Henley Street, Stratford-upon-Avon.*

He had married well, too. In 1557 his bride was Mary Arden, daughter of his father's old landlord, who had died the year before. It was a good match; as Robert's favourite, Mary had inherited substantial money and some farmland in Wilmcote. The first two children, both girls, died as babies. In April 1564, Mary gave birth to her third child, a son named William. The exact date of his birth, like so much else about his life, is disputed. He was certainly baptized at Holy Trinity Church on 26 April, as the Parish Register tells us. Tradition says he was born on 23 April, which, by a happy coincidence, is also the Day of St George, the patron saint of England.

Bubonic plague killed thousands in Elizabethan England. Luckily the 1564 outbreak in Stratford did not kill Shakespeare.

William was fortunate to survive. In the 1564 Burial Register, there is an ominous note on 11 July: 'Here begins the plague'. Bubonic plague swept the country in devastating waves: in this outbreak, 200 people died in Stratford before the end of the year. Luckily it did not reach the Shakespeares' house and William lived on. Other children followed: Gilbert (who was to become

a London haberdasher), Joan (the longest lived), Anne and Richard, who died young, and Edmund, who grew up to be a London actor like his brother.

There are no documents to tell us how William spent his boyhood, but we can make intelligent guesses about certain points. He probably had a fairly privileged life as son of an important citizen. For a time, John continued to prosper, his career reaching its height in 1568 when he became High Bailiff (or Mayor) of Stratford, and applied, unsuccessfully at this time, to the Heralds' College in London for the coat-of-arms of a gentleman. No doubt he and his son enjoyed the ceremonial connected with his position; wearing his scarlet, furred robe, he was escorted to official functions, fairs or markets by buff-uniformed sergeants, carrying maces.

The many references to the Bible or the Prayer Book in the plays tell us that the Church was an important part of William's upbringing, as it was for all Elizabethans. The government compelled church attendance, determined to re-establish the Protestant faith after the Catholic revival under Queen Mary I.

Shakespeare's first contact with plays probably came

As a boy, Shakespeare almost certainly saw actors perform at Stratford Guildhall. Here Cattermole imagines a company of strolling players rehearsing in the woods near Stratford, while William looks on.

A sixteenth-century morality play, like those the young Shakespeare must have seen at the Guildhall.

at the Guildhall, regularly visited by touring acting companies from 1568 onwards. One of his father's duties was to grant licences to such visiting groups, and one of his privileges was to sit with his family in the front row at performances. The plays themselves were mostly moralities, simple dramas: 'godly, learned and fruitful', containing some religious message, but also enlivened by 'pleasant mirth and pastime' and vivid special effects that would impress an imaginative boy.

Shakespeare's formal education, after 'Petty School' where he learned his letters, was certainly at Stratford Grammar School, although there is no written record of his attendance there. Its recently opened schoolroom above the Guildhall was only a quarter of a mile from Henley Street. Highly qualified masters gave the New King's School a good reputation but its regime was

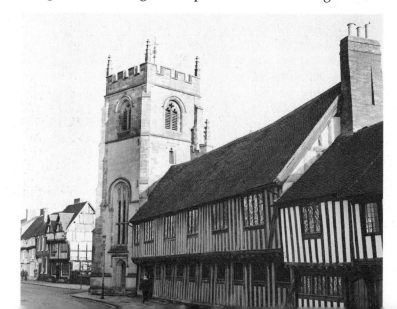

Shakespeare probably attended Stratford Grammar School, which was near his home.

harsh. Boys endured a long, tedious day from 6 am to 5 pm, with a 2 hour midday break. This schooling went on 6 days a week, with rare holidays when a boy might enjoy 'his home and sporting place'. No wonder a boy carved a protest in Latin on one of the school desks: 'Nothing comes from working hard.' Lines in the plays seem to show Shakespeare's distaste for school:

> . . . The whining schoolboy with his satchel
> And shining morning face, creeping like snail
> Unwillingly to school.
>
> (*As You Like It*, II, vii)

> Love goes toward love as schoolboys from their books,
> But love from love, toward school with heavy looks.
>
> (*Romeo and Juliet*, II, ii)

Above the Guildhall, where John Shakespeare attended town council meetings, was the single classroom of the Grammar School. It is still used as a classroom today.

The curriculum was still based almost entirely on Latin. The pupil began with Lily's Latin Grammar, a 200-page pamphlet that he learned by heart, before moving on to simple texts. Much of the work was spoken rather than written; in the picture of Sir Hugh Evans teaching William in *The Merry Wives of Windsor*, Shakespeare gives us a comic version of the teaching style. In the upper forms, pupils were forbidden to speak English at school, as everything had to be done in Latin. Senior boys composed Latin speeches and studied Roman poets: Ovid's *Metamorphoses* remained Shakespeare's lifelong favourite. Work was demanding and the boy William learned much more than the 'small Latin' that Ben Jonson attributed to him.

Shakespeare may not have completed his school course. In 1576, a sudden change came in John Shakespeare's fortunes. Possibly he had some accident or illness that reduced his activity, or he suffered some

Elizabethan school life, with its long hours and frequent use of the birch, was harsh. In his plays, Shakespeare sometimes shows his distaste for schooling.

religious persecution, in that he may have returned to Catholicism, while living in a fiercely Protestant society. He began to miss Council meetings, although he was kindly treated by his fellows, and then he ran into debt, and sold some of his land to obtain cash.

Shakespeare's first biographer of 1709, Nicholas Rowe, claimed that it was these misfortunes – 'the narrowness of his circumstances and the want of his assistance at home' – that made John remove William from school to help him in the shop. Certainly, references to leather craft in the plays show an expert knowledge. A story, collected by John Aubrey in the seventeenth century, shows him working for his father:

> I have been told heretofore by some of the neighbours, that when he was a boy he exercised his father's trade, but when he killed a calf he would do it in high style, and make a speech.
>
> (John Aubrey, *Brief Lives*, 1681)

The next certain reference to Shakespeare concerns his apparently hasty marriage. In the summer of 1582, William, then aged 18, was courting a local woman, 26-year-old Anne Hathaway, who came from a prosperous family living at Hewlands Farm (now preserved as Anne Hathaway's Cottage) at Shottery, a mile across the fields from Henley Street.

> *An Elizabethan love song*
>
> When as the rye reach to the chin
> And chopcherry, chopcherry ripe within,
> Strawberries swimming in the cream,
> And schoolboys swimming in the stream;
> Then Oh, then Oh, then Oh, my true love said,
> Till that time came again
> She could not live a maid.
>
> (George Peele, 1595)

By August, Anne was pregnant. This may not have been as scandalous as it seems, as the couple may have had a 'pre-contract' or 'troth-plight', carried out before witnesses virtually as a civil wedding. For a church marriage, banns had to be read three times before the actual ceremony. Religious law prevented the reading of banns from 2 December to 13 January. Shakespeare therefore had to apply to the Bishop of Worcester for a special licence. Two farmer friends of Anne's also signed a bond to swear there was nothing irregular about the match. The marriage itself was not recorded but was probably celebrated at Temple Grafton or Luddington, where the bride had connections.

Anne then moved into the spacious Henley Street house, where, in May 1583, she gave birth to a daughter, Susanna. The twins, Hamnet and Judith, named after some Stratford friends of William, were born in 1585.

Anne is a shadowy figure. We know only that she outlived her husband, dying in 1623. A tribute to her may survive. One of the sonnets, perhaps a very early one, seems to play on her name (Hathaway/hate away). The poet's 'love' whispers 'I hate', softening the phrase by adding 'not you':

> 'I hate' from hate away she threw
> And sav'd my life, saying 'not you'.

(Sonnet 145)

How Shakespeare might have left Stratford. At the end of Clopton Bridge, he takes leave of his wife, Anne, his daughter, Susanna, and the twins Hamnet and Judith.

From the birth of the twins to 1592, when Shakespeare is first recorded as a writer and actor in London, there is a gap in the documentation that scholars call 'the lost years'. Traditions and theories have filled this gap. Some people think that, as he displays so much knowledge of the law in his plays, Shakespeare must have been a lawyer's clerk in Stratford – but no signature of his appears on any local legal paper. John Aubrey heard he had been 'in his younger years a schoolmaster in the country': could he have acted as private tutor in a great house? Others see him as 'Sergeant Shakespeare', serving with the Earl of Leicester against the Spanish in the Netherlands. His vivid pictures of Italian life lead other theorists to say that he might have travelled there at this time.

During the 'lost years', Shakespeare might have acted as private tutor in an aristocratic household.

The most colourful legend is the deer-stealing episode: his poaching of Sir Thomas Lucy's deer at Charlecote Park, it is said, brought him such trouble that he was forced to leave Stratford.

He had, by a misfortune common enough to young fellows, fallen into ill company; and amongst them, some that made a frequent practice of deer stealing, engaged him with them more than once in robbing a park that belonged to Sir Thomas Lucy of Charlecote, near Stratford. For this he was prosecuted by that gentleman, as he thought, somewhat too severely; and in order to revenge that ill usage, he made a ballad upon him ... It is said to have been so very bitter that it redoubled the prosecution against him to that degree that he was obliged to leave his business and family in Warwickshire for some time, and shelter himself in London.

(Nicholas Rowe, *Life of Shakespeare*, 1709)

The most celebrated legend about Shakespeare claims that he was caught poaching deer in Charlecote Park and was brought before Sir Thomas Lucy.

Shakespeare's high standing in the theatre by 1592 suggests that he must have been learning his craft for several years previously. The Lea Hall theory claims that he became an actor even before his marriage. When wealthy Alexander Houghton of Lea Hall, near Preston in Lancashire, made his will in 1581, he mentioned a 'William Shakeshafte', apparently 'a player . . . now dwelling with me'. There are many attractive coincidences in the theory – one of William's schoolmasters came from this district; the Stanleys, great patrons of the stage, were friends of the Houghtons – but it is now largely discredited: the size of the legacy to Shakeshafte suggests he was too old to be the Stratford William.

Travelling companies of players performed in galleried inn yards, which became the models for permanent theatres.

It is more likely that Shakespeare was drawn towards London by one of the visiting acting companies – 'these glorious vagabonds . . . swooping it in their glaring satin suits' as one writer described them – that came to Stratford in 1586-7. The Queen's Company may have been one man short when it came to the town, one actor having killed another in a quarrel. It has been suggested that Shakespeare filled the gap, returning to London with them. Or did he simply, like his friend Richard Field who became a London printer, go to the capital to seek his fortune? It was a good time to do so: he was 23 years old, and the Elizabethan theatre was about to enter a golden age of creativity.

3 London and the Theatres

In the 1580s, London, with its 150,000 inhabitants, had become one of the wonders of Europe. Its prosperity had increased as war damaged its continental rivals, and was symbolized by the great three-masted trading ships that sailed up to its very heart. 'Silver-streaming Thames' was a kind of highway: thousands of river boatmen invited you 'Eastward Ho!' or 'Westward Ho!' Sometimes the Queen herself took to the water in her magnificent Royal Barge. London Bridge, covered with buildings from end to end, was quite extraordinary. A Swiss doctor, visiting England, wondered at the traitors'

The Thames, with its busy merchant ship traffic, seen in J. C. Visscher's panorama of London (1616).

A close-up of the Bridge Gate with its gruesome display of traitors' heads.

Below *St Paul's Church and the South Bank in Visscher's panorama.*

heads stuck on poles over its southern entrance.

At the top of one tower almost in the centre of the bridge were stuck on tall stakes more than thirty skulls of noblemen who had been executed and beheaded for treason and for other reasons. And their descendants are accustomed to boast of this, themselves even pointing out to one their ancestors' heads on this same bridge, believing that they will be esteemed the more because their antecedents were of such high descent that they could even covet the crown, but being too weak to attain it were executed for rebels; thus they make an honour for themselves of what was set up to be a disgrace and an example.

Thomas Platter, *Platter's Travels* (1599)

The Tower of London, oldest and grimmest of London's sights, was still in use as a prison and, on Tower Hill, as a place of execution.

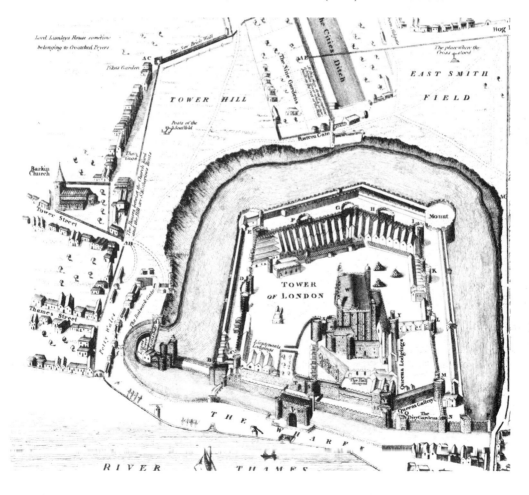

The City itself, still walled, had more than a hundred churches whose spires cut the skyline 'like bristling reeds'. Over all loomed the bulk of old St Paul's Church with its mighty tower. Its atmosphere was far from holy: the central aisle, called Paul's Walk, was a place for business and social display – 'the noise in it is like that of bees, a strange humming or buzz, mixed of walking, tongues and feet.' Outside in the Cathedral Close were the shops of the publishing trade: many of Shakespeare's published works carried the imprint of St Paul's Churchyard.

The Tower of London was the oldest and grimmest of the sights of London. Traitor's Gate, leading to the Bloody Tower, was still in frequent use. Executions on Tower Hill, like those at Tyburn, drew huge crowds. One executioner took a pride in cutting out his victim's heart to show it, still beating, to the dying man.

Public executions were a hideous aspect of the violent Elizabethan era.

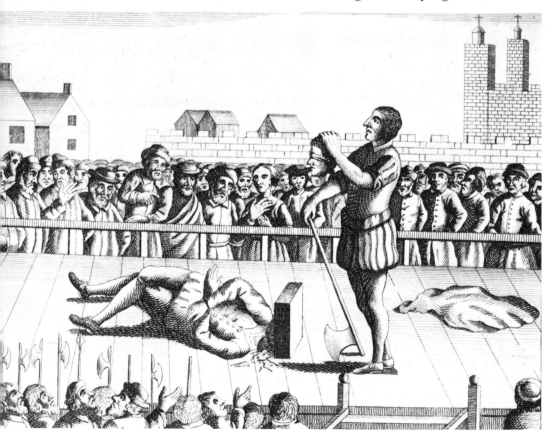

London was a noisy place, with its street cries ('What do you lack?'), its many bells, its traffic that, wrote Dekker, made 'such a thundering as if the world ran upon wheels'. It was lively, too, 'brimful of curiosities', said Platter. He enjoyed the music everywhere, and the many taverns, where he first saw tobacco: 'I am told the inside of one man's veins after death was found to be covered in soot just like a chimney'.

Beyond the City wall to the west, you came to the Inns of Court, a kind of university for prospective lawyers. By the river were the great houses and terraced gardens of leading noblemen, and beyond them lay Whitehall Royal Palace, and Westminster.

In the late 1580s, Queen Elizabeth was at the height of her power. A Spanish-inspired plot to assassinate her and put her rival, Mary Queen of Scots, on the throne had been defeated and Mary executed. King Philip II's huge Armada, which threatened invasion, was scattered and defeated in 1588. The splendour of Court was a symbol of Elizabeth's power and the security she gave

London inns were lively places, famous for their hospitality and the music provided for guests.

The execution of Mary Queen of Scots in 1587 marked the end of Spanish plots to take the English throne from Elizabeth.

The poet Sir Philip Sidney was a favourite of the Queen.

When Shakespeare arrived in London, Queen Elizabeth I was at the height of her splendour and power.

the nation.

Literature flourished at Queen Elizabeth's Court. Royal patronage could give writers large financial rewards for work that pleased or flattered the Queen. Her aristocratic favourites – writers themselves, like Sir Walter Raleigh or Sir Philip Sidney – mirrored Elizabeth's splendour by acting as patrons to poets of humbler origin: Christopher Marlowe, Edmund Spenser, Michael Drayton. Yet it was in drama, often despised as 'the penny knave's delight', that the age produced its most enduring triumphs.

Below *Elizabeth's 'progresses', her tours of England, were marked by spectacular entertainments like this at Elvetsham, Hampshire in 1591.*

Two strands of development came together to make this flowering. There was the popular drama, descended from the old mystery and morality plays but now almost entirely secular. There were stories of all kinds, a cheerful confusion of classical legends, Bible episodes, fragments of ancient or modern history and the latest murder or execution. Audiences loved special effects: a king's pageant with stirring drums, a painted canvas dragon, and blood (Thomas Heywood, a dramatist who wrote 240 plays, described how actors used bladders of pigs' blood under their shirts to explode in fights, and how animals' entrails were used to give realism in stage executions by disembowelling). The popular audience, wrote another playwright, Stephen Gosson, enjoyed 'weeping and mourning' and, by contrast, 'wonderful laughter, shouting together with one voice'.

Thomas Kyd's The Spanish Tragedy *of 1587 was one of the first major dramatic successes of the Elizabethan era. Hieronimo discovers his son Horatio hanging dead in the garden, while the murderers try to silence Horatio's lover.*

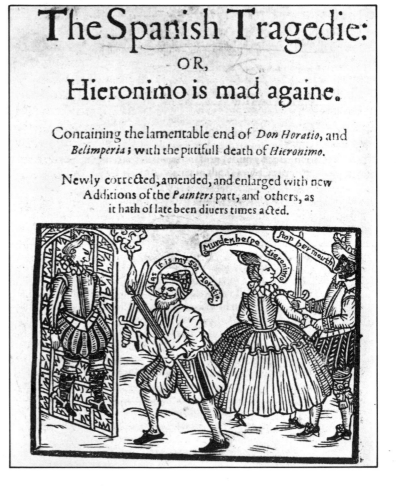

34

The second type of drama was that of clever young men-about-town; students at the Inns of Court, graduates of Oxford and Cambridge, or ex-Grammar School pupils, who had read the plays and the dramatic criticism of ancient Rome and Greece, and wished to imitate them. The first English success in this classical style, using a new medium, blank verse, was *Gorboduc* (1561) by Thomas Norton and Thomas Sackville. Yet the popular theatre, with its hungry market for plays, attracted the 'University Wits', 'the rhyming and scribbling crew'. The grandeur and order of the classics combined with the energy of the popular stage, produced the first outstanding successes of Elizabethan drama: *Tamburlaine* by Christopher Marlowe and *The Spanish Tragedy* by Thomas Kyd, both produced in 1587. Marlowe's 'mighty line', the first great dramatic blank verse, was a powerful contrast with that of other dramatists. Audiences thrilled to the scenes where Tamburlaine harnesses two captive kings to pull him in his chariot, or where the Governor of Babylon, hung up in chains, is shot at with live bullets. Kyd's play, the first of the revenge genre, was full of horror, with three suicides and six hideous murders.

Until 1576, actors had no permanent theatres. They performed in town halls, great houses or inn yards, like those of the Bull, Bel Savage or Cross Keys, where the audience stood in the courtyard, while more expensive seats were provided in the galleries around it. However, the actors had to pay rent to the innkeeper, losing part

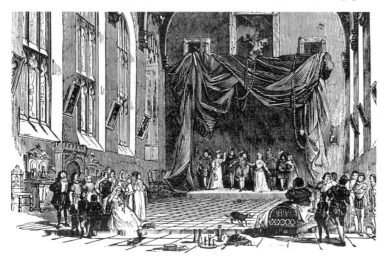

Before permanent theatres were built, travelling players performed in town halls and great houses.

of their profit. Moreover, the City authorities disapproved of the stage 'like a sink in a town where all the filth doth run ... Its common haunters are for the most part the very scum, rascality and baggage of the people.' Several times in the 1590s, the Lord Mayor of London sent the Queen petitions against plays that were, he thought, 'nothing but profane fables, lascivious matters, cozening devices and scurrilous behaviours'. Fortunately the Queen enjoyed plays and encouraged actors. When, in the early 1570s, the government allowed daily performances of plays, it became economically possible to build purpose-designed theatres.

James Burbage, carpenter turned actor, was the pioneer. He opened his Theatre in 1576, in the Liberty of Holywell in Shoreditch, north of the City. 'Liberties' were areas of land formerly owned by the Church and confiscated by the Crown: within or outside the City walls, they escaped the control of the Lord Mayor. Although it was a long walk to Holywell, the Theatre was at once popular and profitable: 'thither run the people thick and threefold', complained a London preacher.

The Queen was a generous patron of the drama. This is Cattermole's idea of how Shakespeare's company might have looked as they acted at Court.

A second theatre, the Curtain, opened nearby in 1577. This was described by Platter in 1599:

The places are built in such a way that they act on a raised scaffold, and everyone can well see everything. However, there are separate galleries and places, where one sits more pleasantly and better, therefore also pays more.

(Thomas Platter, *Travels in England*, 1599)

Few pictures survive of sixteenth-century stage performances. Here a play is staged in the hall of a great house.

Opposite *The Dutch writer, Johannes de Witt, described and drew the Swan Theatre in 1596. The 'mimorun aedes' is the dressing room; the 'ingressus' the entrance.*

He noted the social mixture of the audience, reflected in the scale of charges giving access to various parts of the theatre. A top person might have a more expensive seat behind, or even on, the stage, 'where he not only sees everything well but can also be seen.'

From the 1580s, the south bank of the Thames at Southwark was to become another theatrical centre. The bear-baiting arena was already there, and nearby, in 1587, the enterprising Elizabethan businessman, Philip Henslowe, built the Rose Theatre. Here his son-in-law, the great actor, Edward Alleyn, with his 'furious gestures' and 'bent brows', drew the crowds to *Tamburlaine*. The Swan also opened here in 1596. A Dutch writer, Johannes de Witt, described it:

> Of all the theatres the largest and most magnificent is that of which the sign is the swan . . . it accommodates in its seats three thousand persons and is built of a mass of flintstones, and supported by wooden columns painted in such excellent imitation of marble that it is able to deceive even the most cunning.

He also made a sketch of the Swan, a precious document as it is our only contemporary drawing of an Elizabethan theatre interior.

An Elizabethan play performance. The more expensive seats were in the balcony, whilst the 'groundlings' paid less to stand in front of the stage.

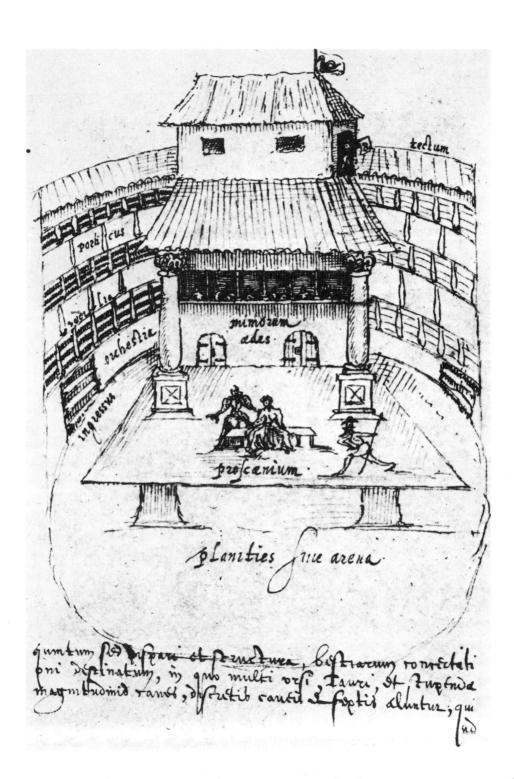

tectum

porti cus

sedilia

orchestra

mimorum aedes

ingressus

proscænium.

planities siue arena.

quintum est visum et structura, bestiarum concitatati
oni destinatum, in quo multi ursi, tauri, et stupenda
magnitudinis canes, distinctis cauis et septis aluntur, qui

39

4 The First London Successes

Shakespeare's London career probably began at the north suburban theatres. An anecdote claims that he began work as a horse-minder.

> ... his first expedient was to wait at the door of the playhouse and hold the horses of those that had no servants, that they might be ready again after the performance. In this office he became so conspicuous for his care and readiness, that in a short time every man as he alighted called for Will Shakespeare ... This was the first dawn of better fortune.
>
> (Samuel Johnson, Edition of 1765)

Another tradition claims that his first theatrical post was prompter's attendant, reminding actors of their entrances, but, speculated his early biographers, his conversation was 'so fine and so acute' that he was soon promoted to actor and writer.

The first definite reference that ends the obscurity of the 'lost years' and shows his rapid rise to success comes from one of the 'University Wits', Thomas Nashe. He comments admiringly on the dramatic impact of the rise and tragic fall of the English general, Lord Talbot, who appears in Shakespeare's early history play, *Henry VI*.

> How it would have joyed brave Talbot (the terror of the French) to think that after he had lain two hundred years in his tomb, he should triumph again on the stage, and

Opposite *Dr Samuel Johnson was a brilliant eighteenth-century editor and critic of Shakespeare.*

41

The failed playwright, Robert Greene, wrote bitterly about Shakespeare's success. This pamphlet of 1598 shows him writing in poverty just before his death, morbidly wearing his own shroud.

have his bones new embalmed with the tears of ten thousand spectators . . .

(Thomas Nashe, *Pierce Penniless*, 1592)

Another more envious comment comes from a failed writer, Robert Greene. He resented Shakespeare because he was an actor: one of the – 'rude grooms' – who paid writers – 'men of such rare wits' – small fees for plays, yet made large profits themselves. Greene was also furious because Shakespeare's plays had displaced his own on the stage.

There is an upstart crow, beautified with our feathers, that with his 'Tiger's heart wrapped in a player's hide' supposes he is as well able to bombast out a blank verse as the best of you; and, being an absolute Johannes Factotum [John-do-everything], is in his own conceit the only Shake-scene in a country.

(Robert Greene, *Greene's Groatsworth of wit*, 1592)

A PLAYER.

AN AUTHOR.

Greene puns on Shakespeare's name and parodies a line: 'O tiger's heart wrapped in a woman's hide', from *Henry VI part 3*, where the Duke of York, about to be murdered, speaks bitterly to cruel Queen Margaret.

Shakespeare left no convenient list to show the date order of his plays. Henslowe's business diary of 1592–1602 is helpful to us in this respect. It is the most valuable of all Elizabethan stage records, listing plays performed at the Rose and noting whether they were new and how much money they made. What he called *Harey the VI* (probably part 1) was the success of 1592–3. In this, and

In the name of god Amen begininge the 19 of febreary my
lord stranges mene as foloweth
1591

Rd at fryer bacone the 19 of febreary 1591 Satterday — xvijs vjd
Rd at mvlomvrco the 20 of febreary 1591 — xxixs
Rd at orlando the 21 of febreary 1591 — xvjs vjd
Rd at spanes comodye donne oracoe the 23 of febreary 1591 — xiijs vjd
Rd at syr John mandevell the 24 of febreary 1591 — xijs vjd
Rd at harey of cornwell the 25 of febreary 1591 — xxxijs
Rd at the Jewe of malta the 26 of febreary 1591 — l
Rd at clorys & orgasto the 28 of febreary 1591 — xviijs
Rd at mvlamvlluco the 29 of febreary 1591 — xxxiiijs
Rd at poope Jone the 1 of marche 1591 — xvs
Rd at matchavell the 2 of marche 1591 — xiijs
Rd at harey the vj the 3 of marche 1591 — iijli xvjs 8
Rd at bendo & Richardo the 4 of marche 1591 — xvjs
Rd at iiij playes in one the 6 of marche 1591 — xxxjs 6
Rd at harey the vj the 7 of marche 1591 — iijli
Rd at the lockinglasse the 8 of marche 1591 — vijs
Rd at senobia the 9 of marche 1591 — xxijs vjd
Rd at the Jewe of malta the 10 of marche 1591 — lvjs 6
Rd at harey the vj the 11 of marche 1591 — xxxxvijs vjd
Rd at the comodey of doneoracio the 13 of marche 1591 — xxviijs
Rd at Jeronymo the 14 of marche 1591 — iijli xjs vjd
Rd at harey the 16 of marche 1591 — xxxjs 6
Rd at mvlo mvlloco the 17 of marche 1591 — xxviijs vjd
Rd at the Jewe of malta the 18 of marche 1591 — xxxxijs vjd
Rd at Jeronymo the 20 of marche 1591 — xxxviijs
Rd at constantine the 21 of marche 1591 — xxijs
Rd at Q. Jerusalem the 22 of marche 1591 — xviijs
Rd at harey of cornwell the 23 of marche 1591 — xxxijs 6
Rd at fryer bacone the 25 of marche 1591 — xxxvijs vjd
Esterdaye Rd at the lockinglasse the 27 of marche 1591 — ls
Rd at harey the vj the 28 of marche 1591 — iijli vij 8
Rd at mvlamvlluco the 29 of marche 1591 — iijli vijs
Rd at doneoracio the 30 of marche 1591 — xxxixs
Rd at Jeronymo the 31 of marche 1591 — iijli
Rd at mandevell the 1 of aprell 1591 — xiiijs 6
Rd at matchavell the 3 of aprell 1591 — xviijs
Rd at the Jewe of malta the 4 of aprell 1591 — xxxxvjs
Rd at harey the vj the 5 of aprell 1591 — xxxxvijs
Rd at brandymer the 6 of aprell 1591 — xxijs 6
Rd at Jeronymo the 7 of aprell 1591 — xxxiijs ..o..10..w
Rd at mvlomvloco the 8 of aprell 1591 — xxxiijs

Opposite *Philip Henslowe, an Elizabethan businessman and theatre pioneer, left an account book noting performances at his Rose Theatre. These entries note that Henry VI ('Harey the VI) was so popular that it was performed fifteen times in 1592–3.*

Richard III, the hunch-backed king who ruthlessly murdered his way to power.

in its other parts, which display the power struggles of the Wars of the Roses, Shakespeare adapted and enriched a favourite source: Ralph Holinshed's *Chronicles* of British history, published in 1577.

From Sir Thomas More's Tudor-biased version of the story, as incorporated in Hollinshed's *Chronicle* and that of Edward Hall (1542), came the outline of *Richard III*. The hunch-backed king, who laughs as he murders his way to the throne, has always attracted leading actors

Now is the winter of our discontent
Made glorious summer by this sun of York;
And all the clouds that lower'd upon our house
In the deep bosom of the ocean buried.
Now are our brows bound with victorious wreaths;
Our bruised arms hung up for monuments:
Our stern alarums chang'd to merry meetings,
Our dreadful marches to delightful measures.
Grim-visag'd war hath smooth'd his wrinkled front . . .
But I, that am not shaped for sportive tricks
Nor made to court an amorous looking-glass,
I that am rudely stamped and want love's majesty
To strut before a wanton ambling nymph . . .
Deformed, unfinished, sent before my time
Into this breathing world scarce half made up –
And that so lamely and unfashionable
That dogs bark at me as I halt by them –
Why, I in this weak piping time of peace
Have no delight to pass away the time.
Unless to spy my shadow in the sun
And descant on mine own deformity.
And therefore since I cannot prove a lover
To entertain these fair well-spoken days,
I am determined to prove a villain . . .

(*Richard III*, I, i)

Henslowe noted another early success, the grim tragedy, *Titus Andronicus*. A story of double revenge, it is full of extreme horrors: Titus has a hand hacked off; his sons' heads are carried in to him; his daughter, Lavinia, is raped, and her attackers cut off her hands and cut out her tongue; Titus slits their throats, while Lavinia catches the blood in a bowl; and he serves their flesh to their mother in a pie!

In very different vein, Shakespeare used the Roman writer, Plautus, as a model for *The Comedy of Errors*, presented in 1594 at a wild Christmas revel at the Inns of Court: 'So that night was begun and continued to the end in nothing but confusion and errors'. With its two sets of twins, its puns, its vivid language (Nell, the kitchen maid, is 'spherical, like a globe'), it can still, as it did at an early nineteenth-century performance, seen by a friend of the poet, Keats, make 'an audience in their laughter roll about like waves'.

Opposite Titus Andronicus *contains many grotesque horrors. The Roman Emperor forces Titus to lose a hand to demonstrate his love for his sons: here Aaron the Moor cuts off Titus's hand.*

Here people are shown fleeing from the towns to avoid the plague.

In 1592, a severe outbreak of plague struck London. The black rats whose fleas carried the plague bacillus found good breeding grounds in the 'filthy alleys' of London's overcrowded suburban slums. Infected families were locked in their houses; ten thousand perished in 1593. City preachers blamed the theatres for the sickness: 'The cause of plagues is sin ... and the cause of sin are plays; therefore the cause of plagues are plays.' The government, knowing that crowds did spread infection, was for once ready to listen to the Lord Mayor and forbade 'all manner of concourse and public meetings of the people at plays, bear-baitings, bowlings and other like assemblies.' The theatres remained shut for two years, a serious blow to the acting companies, and a disaster to the writers: their market had gone.

Enforced leisure apparently made Shakespeare turn to poetry. A narrative poem, *Venus and Adonis*, based on an episode from his favourite Latin book, Ovid's *Metamorphoses*, was published in 1593 by his Stratford friend, Richard Field, now a London publisher. It became immensely popular, going through ten editions in Shakespeare's lifetime. 'The younger sort takes much

Opposite *Plague closed the theatres of London in 1592. Victims were buried in mass graves.*

49

delight in Shakespeare's *Venus and Adonis*', wrote one enthusiast in 1598, while to another the poet became 'Sweet Mr Shakespeare. I'll have his picture in my study ... and lay his *Venus and Adonis* under my pillow.' Its descriptive episodes can still appeal to the young reader, as in this picture of Wat, a hare hunted by hounds:

Opposite
Shakespeare dedicated his narrative poems to Henry Wriothesley, Earl of Southampton.

> Then shalt thou see the dew-bedabbled wretch
> Turn and return, indenting with the way.
> Each envious briar his heavy legs doth scratch;
> Each shadow makes him stop, each murmur stay;
>   For misery is trodden on by many,
>   And, being low, never relieved by any.

(Venus and Adonis, 703–708)

Shakespeare dedicated this poem, 'the first heir of my invention', to Henry Wriothesley, Earl of Southampton, a 19-year-old rising star at Court: 'no young man more outstanding in learning'. 'If your honour seem but pleased,' wrote the poet, 'I account myself highly praised, and vow to take advantage of all idle hours, till I have honoured you with some graver labour.' This promised second poem was *The Rape of Lucrece*, based on the story of the cruel Roman king's brutal attack on Lucretia, a woman famous for her virtue. This proved even more popular than his first poem. The dedication to Southampton is warmer and more personal ('The love I dedicate to your Lordship is without end') – perhaps he had now met his patron and been given reward for his work (one story says he received the then huge sum of £1,000). These published poems gave Shakespeare fresh fame. Another writer, Richard Barnfield, thought him a poet:

> Whose Venus, and whose Lucrece, sweet and chaste,
> Thy name in fame's immortal book have placed.

At this time, too, when the fashion for writing sonnets flourished with Sir Philip Sidney's sonnet sequence *Astrophel and Stella* (1591), Shakespeare wrote his sequence of 'sugared sonnets', intended only to circulate among his private friends. Fortunately for us, they were later collected and published, probably without his permission, in 1609.

TO . THE . ONLIE . BEGETTER . OF .
THESE . INSVING . SONNETS .
M^r. W. H. ALL . HAPPINESSE .
AND . THAT . ETERNITIE .
PROMISED .

BY .

OVR . EVER-LIVING . POET .

WISHETH .

THE . WELL-WISHING .
ADVENTVRER . IN .
SETTING .
FORTH .

T. T.

Shakespeare's sonnet sequence contains 154 poems. Each may be read on its own, but together they tell something of a story of a three-sided love affair between the poet, the 'fair friend' (a handsome young man?) and a 'dark lady'. There are many unanswered mysteries about the sonnets that have fascinated scholars. Are the main characters real people? Who is 'Mr W. H.', to whom the printed book is dedicated as 'the only begetter of these ensuing sonnets'? Whatever the riddles, readers have always loved the sonnets, not only as complete units, but for the many thought-provoking and beautiful ideas and comparisons they contain:

> Shall I compare thee to a summer's day?
> Thou art more lovely and more temperate.
> Rough winds do shake the darling buds of May,
> And summer's lease hath all too short a date . . .
>
> (Sonnet 18)

> When to the sessions of sweet silent thought
> I summon up remembrance of things past . . .
>
> (Sonnet 30)

> Like as the waves make towards the pebbled shore,
> So do our minutes hasten to their end . . .
>
> (Sonnet 60)

> Three winters cold
> Have from the forests shook three summers' pride;
> Three beauteous springs to yellow autumn turned
> In process of the seasons have I seen,
> Three April perfumes in three hot Junes burned
> Since first I saw you fresh . . .
>
> (Sonnet 104)

Although Shakespeare abandoned a promising career as a poet when the theatres re-opened in 1594, he composed many fresh, delightful songs for his plays. The sophisticated comedy, *Love's Labours Lost*, with its elaborate play on language and style, possibly dates from these plague years, composed perhaps for some private aristocratic entertainment at a great house. The play ends with a song, whose homely but striking images, in

Opposite *The mysterious dedication in the 1609 edition of the sonnets. There are many theories about the identity of Mr W.H.*

marked contrast to the elaboration of the play, create a vivid picture of the Elizabethan countryside in winter and show a very different side to Shakespeare's genius as a poet.

> When icicles hang by the wall,
> And Dick the shepherd blows his nail,
> And Tom bears logs into the hall,
> And milk comes frozen home in pail;
> When blood is nipped, and ways be foul,
> Then nightly sings the staring owl:
> Tu-whit, tu-whoo! – a merry note,
> While greasy Joan doth keel the pot.
>
> (*Love's Labours Lost*, V, ii)

Love's Labours Lost, *sold to the printers in 1597–8 during a difficult period for Shakespeare's company, was the first play to be published with his name attached.*

A PLEASANT Conceited Comedie CALLED, Loues labors loft.

As it vvas prefented before her Highnes this laft Chriftmas.

Newly corrected and augmented By W. Shakefpere.

5 The Late Elizabethan Years

When the London theatres re-opened in the spring of 1594, Shakespeare had no serious rival as a dramatist – Christopher Marlowe had been killed in a fight about a disputed bill at a Deptford tavern in May 1593. The years of triumph now began.

Shakespeare's greatest rival, Christopher Marlowe, was killed in a tavern brawl in Deptford near London in 1593.

Shakespeare would have had little time to write: the Elizabethan theatre was an impatient institution that would not allow a writer to 'lie in childbed one and thirty weeks' to produce 'three bad lines'. His fellow actors tell us that he worked astonishingly swiftly and accurately: 'We scarce have received from him a blot in his papers'. When a play was finished, it had to be licensed by the Queen's Master of Revels to make sure it did not contain anti-government material. The manuscript, backed to make it a 'book', was jealously guarded by the company as there were no copyright laws. A copier

wrote out the actors' parts, with prompts and cues, on six-inch wide strips of paper that could be unrolled as the actor worked. Play-books were only published in very hard times for the company, or from stolen or half-remembered texts. That is why most Elizabethan plays have been lost. Writers sold their plays outright to the company, not benefiting from any steady success. But Shakespeare, as a company 'sharer' was entitled to part of the profits, those pennies that poured into the gatherers' bags at theatre doors. In this way, his wealth grew steadily.

Shakespeare's rise to fame in the 1590s was summed up by a young writer, Francis Meres, who, in 1598, published *Palladio Tamia: Wit's Treasury*, in which Shakespeare was praised as one of several writers by whom 'the English tongue is mightily enriched and gorgeously invested in rare ornaments.' Meres then presents his invaluable list of Shakespeare's plays to date, including one mysterious lost play, *Love's Labours Won* (perhaps he meant *The Taming of the Shrew*, not mentioned elsewhere). Meres mentions other writers, but reserves his special praise for Shakespeare: 'The Muses [gods who inspire artists] would speak with Shakespeare's fine-filed phrases, if they could speak English.'

Meres' list includes some of Shakespeare's most popular successes. *A Midsummer Night's Dream* was probably written, about 1594–5, for some fashionable wedding attended by the Queen herself ('A fair vestal thronèd by the west'). Shakespeare blends Greek myth with English folklore to create a magical, dream-like world where 'quick bright things come to confusion'. One of the loveliest, and happiest, of the plays, it is full of exquisite poetry which later poets – such as Milton and Keats – were to imitate.

> I know a bank whereon the wild thyme blows,
> Where oxslips and the nodding violet grows,
> Quite overcanopied with luscious woodbine,
> With sweet musk roses, and with eglantine.
> There sleeps Titania sometime of the night,
> Lulled in these flowers with dances and delight;
> And there the snake throws her enamelled skin,
> Weed wide enough to wrap a fairy in . . .
>
> (*A Midsummer Night's Dream*, II, 1)

William Blake's watercolour painting catches the magic of A Midsummer Night's Dream: *Oberon, Titania and Puck watch a fairy dance.*

In contrast with the delicate scenes of the lovers and fairies are those involving the Athenian workmen, the 'mechanicals'. Bottom has been called Shakespeare's first original dramatic creation. Dr Johnson noted how he made fun of the weaver's claims to be an actor:

> He is for engrossing every part and would exclude his inferiors from all possibility of distinction. He is therefore desirous to play Pyramus, Thisbe, and the Lion at the same time.

> (Samuel Johnson, Edition of 1765)

Romeo and Juliet was adapted from a poem by Arthur Brooke, itself a verse translation of an Italian novel. Shakespeare sharpens the original, cutting the action from months to a week of 'hot days', making Juliet younger, and the 'star-crossed lovers' more obviously hasty and rash. Here he showed his astonishing ability to create a range of living characters. From the first, young people especially have responded to the play's magical poetry, its harsh contrasts of love and hatred, its bitter ironies.

JULIET O, think'st thou we shall ever meet again?
ROMEO I doubt it not, and all these woes shall serve
       For sweet discourses in our times to come.
JULIET O God, I have an ill-divining soul!
       Methinks I see thee, now thou art so low,
       As one dead in the bottom of a tomb.
       Either my eyesight fails, or thou look'st pale.
ROMEO And trust me, love, in my eye so do you.
       Dry sorrow drinks our blood. Adieu, adieu.

(*Romeo and Juliet*, III, v)

The 'star-crossed lovers', Romeo and Juliet, have fascinated young people since they first appeared on stage. This is a still from the Franco Zefferelli film version.

The first printed edition speaks of the 'great applause' that the play had received. Elizabethan anthologies quoted many lines from the play: young enthusiasts, it seemed, could speak 'nought but pure Juliet and Romeo'.

Shakespeare continued his history sequences with another tetralogy, from *Richard II* through the two parts of *Henry IV* to *Henry V*. The darker themes of these plays, depicting the horrors of the power struggle between the Houses of Lancaster and York, were almost submerged by another mighty character, Sir John Falstaff (at first called Oldcastle, until that family objected), the fat, disreputable associate of Prince Hal. 'Unimitable Falstaff', wrote Dr Johnson, is a character 'loaded with faults' yet he 'makes himself necessary to the Prince that despises him by the most pleasing of all qualities, perpetual gaiety, by an unfailing power of exciting laughter.' Falstaff – 'that swollen parcel of humours, that huge bombard of sack [wine], that stuffed cloak-bag of guts, that roasted Maningtree ox with the pudding in his belly' – was loved by all kinds of audiences from the 'groundlings' to the Queen herself. An eighteenth-century story says that she 'was so well pleased with that admirable character ... that she commanded him [Shakespeare] to continue it for one play more, and to show him in love.' The title page of a published edition of *The Merry Wives of Windsor*, where Falstaff again appears, claiming that the play had been 'acted before Her Majesty', might confirm this rumour.

Shakespeare may have begun his career with the Queen's Men (with their incomparable clown, Richard Tarlton, who once made the Queen laugh so much that she ordered his removal from the stage). He may have written freelance for other companies, including Henslowe's. The mists clear with a 1595 reference about a payment by the Master of Court Revels to 'William Kemp, William Shakespeare and Richard Burbage, servants to the Lord Chamberlain.' Henry, Lord Hunsdon, Lord Chamberlain, a cultivated Court official, had championed the actors in their battles with the Mayor of London. His company, which played very often at Court, at his private entertainments and at the Theatre, outstripped even their powerful rivals, the Admiral's Men (patronized by Lord Howard, who had commanded the

Fleet against the Spanish Armada), led by Edward Alleyn at the Rose. Richard Burbage, son of the Theatre's founder, James, created most of Shakespeare's great tragic roles, while Will Kemp was an outstanding comedian.

There are records of Shakespeare as an actor, a demanding life in itself, right through his career. We do not know exactly what parts he played, although anecdotes mention him as the old man, Adam, in *As You Like It*, or as the Ghost in *Hamlet*, or generally in 'kingly parts'. His expertise is reflected in Hamlet's instructions to the company of actors that visit Elsinore:

> Speak the speech, I pray you, as I pronounced it to you – trippingly on the tongue, but if you mouth it, as many of your players do, I had as lief the town crier spoke my lines. Nor do not saw the air too much with your hand, thus, but use all gently ... O, it offends me to the soul to hear a robustious, periwig-pated fellow tear

This Comoedie was first Acted, in the yeere
1598.

By the then L. CHAMBERLAYNE
his Seruants.

The principall Comoedians were.

WILL SHAKESPEARE.	RIC. BVRBADGE.
AVG. PHILIPS.	IOH. HEMINGS.
HEN. CONDEL.	THO. POPE.
WILL. SLYE.	CHA. BEESTON.
WILL. KEMPE.	IOH. DVKE.

With the allowance of the Master of REUELS.

61

a passion to tatters, to very rags, to split the ears of the groundlings ... Suit the action to the word, the word to the action, with this special observance: that you o'erstep not the modesty of nature. For anything so overdone is from the purpose of playing, whose end ... was and is, to hold, as 'twere, the mirror up to nature.

(*Hamlet*, III, ii)

Shylock, the Jewish money-lender in *The Merchant of Venice*, was another of the memorable creations of these years, inspired perhaps by the success of Marlowe's *The Jew of Malta*, and by Elizabethan preoccupation with usury: money-lending which charges interest. There was also the scandal surrounding the supposed attempt to poison the Queen by her physician, Dr Lopez, a Portuguese Jew, falsely accused by the Earl of Essex, and hanged and quartered at Tyburn in 1594. This incident fanned anti-Semitic feeling in England. The ambiguities of Shylock's character (does Shakespeare dislike or pity him?) and the vitality of the language have made the role a classic acting challenge.

I am a Jew. Hath not a Jew eyes? Hath not a Jew hands, organs, dimensions, senses, affections, passions? fed with the same food, hurt with the same weapons, subject to the same diseases, healed by the same means, warmed and cooled by the same winter and summer, as a Christian is? If you prick us, do we not bleed? If you tickle us, do we not laugh? If you poison us, do we not die? and if you wrong us, shall we not revenge?

(*The Merchant of Venice*, III, i)

Shakespeare's working home was in London and he has been traced to various houses where he lodged in the City. Yet his family still lived in Stratford to which, said John Aubrey, 'he was wont to go ... once a year'. One legend claimed that he usually stopped on this journey at an Oxford inn, the Tavern, run by the Davenant family. One of their sons recalled how their favourite guest once gave him a hundred kisses, while another son, William (who became a writer, too, and who liked to claim he was actually Shakespeare's natural son), was so fond of the great man that he would 'fly from school to see him ... running homeward almost out of breath.'

Stratford was where Shakespeare carefully invested his profits from the theatre. His money restored the family fortunes after his father's troubles. John Shakespeare's application for the coat-of-arms of a gentleman was renewed, with his son's support, and was granted in 1596.

Yet Shakespeare's efforts to rebuild family strength and pride received a setback when his only son, Hamnet, then 11 years old, died in August 1596. Although *King John* was written before this time, the lament of Constance for her son, Prince Arthur, has often been noted as a poignantly appropriate epitaph for Hamnet.

In 1596, the College of Arms granted John Shakespeare the coat-of-arms of a gentleman. The crest is on the top left of the document.

Grief fills the room up of my absent child,
Lies in his bed, walks up and down with me,
Puts on his pretty looks, repeats his words,
Remembers me of all his gracious parts,
Stuffs out his vacant garments with his form . . .
My life, my joy, my food, my all the world . . .

(*King John*, III, iv)

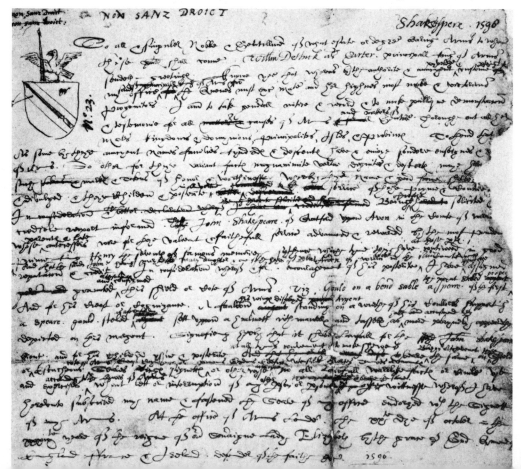

Shakespeare bought New Place, the finest house in Stratford, in 1597. Only the garden survives today.

In 1597, Shakespeare, as if to show his success to local people, bought New Place, the finest house in Stratford. With an impressive three-storey frontage, it stood in spacious gardens, which contained orchards and barns, near the Guild Chapel. The house had fallen into decay but Shakespeare 'repaired and modelled it to his own mind'. He planted the celebrated mulberry tree and, no doubt, pruned the vines for which the house was noted.

Thereafter the records show how Shakespeare gradually extended his investments in goods and land. His old neighbours were impressed by his prosperity. In 1598, Richard Quiney, a Stratford businessman, wrote to his 'loving good friend and countryman, Mr Wm. Shakespeare', to ask for a loan: 'You shall friend me much in helping me out of all the debts I owe in London.' The request was never sent, and so survives as the only letter written to Shakespeare that we have.

In London, the Chamberlain's Men had run into trouble when the lease for the Theatre ran out in 1597. Then James Burbage, the theatrical pioneer, suddenly died. After a long dispute with the landlord, during which the Theatre stood 'unfrequented, in dark silence and vast solitude', Burbage's two sons decided to dismantle the building and to carry the timber across the Thames to a new site near the Rose in Southwark.

The new Globe Theatre, opened in May 1599, was London's finest, 'the glory of the Bank'. In this 'Wooden O', as Shakespeare called it, his greatest plays were to be presented. Exactly what the Globe was like inside, and how plays were actually staged, has been endlessly disputed. We have no interior drawings and only tantalizing glimpses like this of Platter, who went there in September:

> ... after dinner, at about two o'clock, I went with my party across the water; in the straw-thatched house we saw the tragedy of the first Emperor Julius Caesar, very pleasantly performed ... at the end of the play they danced together admirably and exceedingly gracefully, according to their custom.

(Thomas Platter, Travels in England, 1599)

Some evidence can be gained from the surviving construction schedule for the Fortune, the new theatre for the Alleyn–Henslowe 'Admiral's Men', opened in north London in 1600. Although the building was square, it was modelled on 'the late erected playhouse on the Bank'. The schedule gives us the theatre's dimensions and some detail of its stage and rooms, although, sadly, the carpenter's drawing to accompany the notes has not survived.

Although Elizabethan theatre was more aural than visual – that is people listened and let the words create pictures in their imaginations – spectacle was a feature of its stagecraft. Costumes for actors could be splendid to look at. Henslowe's papers mention 'a short velvet cloak, embroidered with gold and gold spangles', and 'a crimson robe striped with gold, faced with ermine' – but there was no attempt at historical accuracy: Shakespeare's Romans wore cloaks, doublets and Tudor hats rather than togas. Henslowe's list of properties includes such strange, colourful items as these:

> i rock, i cage, i tomb, i Hell mouth
> i Old Mahomet's head, i tree of golden apples
> i Golden Fleece, i dragon in Faustus
> i ghost's crown, ii lions' heads, i black dog
> i great horse with his legs

(Henslowe's papers, 1598)

Opposite *A Bankside theatre as seen on Visscher's View of London. Although it is named the Globe, this is probably the Rose. The theatres were cylindrical rather than polygonal, as shown here.*

A reconstruction of a performance at Henslowe's Fortune Theatre.

Stage directions show how ambitious productions could be: 'Let there be a brazen head set in the middle of the place behind the stage, out of which cast flames of fire, drums rumble within', or 'Exit Venus; or if you conveniently can let a chair come down from the top of the stage and draw her up'. Sound effects were important, from the elaborate system of trumpet calls to the rolled cannon ball indicating thunder.

Henry V was possibly the first play produced at the Globe. An adaptation of Holinshed's and Edward Hall's chronicle histories and of older play versions of the story, like *The Famous Victories of Henry the Fifth*, it centres on 'the star of England ... the pattern of princehood', who was a national hero in the popular memory. The Tudor historical vision saw his brief reign as an interlude of stable authority and national stability between hideous periods of civil war. Henry's fine rhetorical speeches are offset by the Chorus's atmospheric scene settings. Here is the night before the battle of Agincourt, as the small English force awaits its confrontation with the huge French army.

> From camp to camp through the foul womb of night
> The hum of either army stilly sounds,
> That the fixed sentinels almost receive
> The secret whispers of each other's watch.
> Fire answers fire, and through their paly flames
> Each battle sees the other's umbered face.
> Steed threatens steed, in high and boastful neighs
> Piercing the night's dull ear, and from the tents
> The armourers, accomplishing the knights,
> With busy hammers closing rivets up,
> Give dreadful note of preparation . . .
>
> (*Henry V*, III, vi)

King Henry V receives the French surrender after the Battle of Agincourt: a still from Laurence Olivier's celebrated 1944 film version.

For *Julius Caesar*, Shakespeare turned from English to Roman history, subtly modifying Sir Thomas North's 1579 translation of Plutarch's *Lives of the Noble Grecians and Romans*. Caesar's murder had often been shown on stage in other play versions, but Shakespeare boldly shifted the centre of interest from Caesar to Brutus, to study the mind of a tormented man whose principles force him to murder his best friend. Of the many striking scenes, perhaps the quarrel of Brutus and Cassius has always seemed particularly dramatic. A contemporary noted its power:

The quarrel of Brutus and Cassius, after their murder of Julius Caesar, has always been a favourite scene with audiences.

So have I seen, when Caesar would appear,
And on the stage at half sword parley were
Brutus and Cassius; O, how the audience
Were ravished, with what wonder they went thence . . .

(Leonard Digges,
Upon Master William Shakespeare, 1636)

After the quarrel, Brutus explains his state of mind to Cassius: his beloved wife Portia has killed herself.

BRUTUS O Cassius, I am sick of many griefs.
CASSIUS Of your philosophy you make no use,
        If you give place to accidental evils.
BRUTUS No man bears sorrow better. Portia is dead.
CASSIUS Ha! Portia?
BRUTUS She is dead.
CASSIUS How scaped I killing when I crossed you so?
        O insupportable and touching loss!
        Upon what sickness?
BRUTUS Impatience of my absence,
        And grief that young Octavius with Mark Antony
        Have made themselves so strong – for with her death
        That tidings came. With this, she fell distraught,
        And, her attendants absent, swallowed fire.
CASSIUS And died so?
BRUTUS   Even so.

(*Julius Caesar*, IV, iii)

Rosalind and Orlando in As You Like It. *In Shakespeare's time, Rosalind would have been a boy actor playing a girl who in turn dresses as a boy.*

It is remarkable that, in the brilliant comedies of these late Elizabethan years – *Much Ado About Nothing*, *As You Like It*, *Twelfth Night* – Shakespeare relied on boy actors to interpret such demanding roles as 'sweet' Beatrice, 'heavenly' Rosalind, and charming Viola. Women did not act until after Charles II's Restoration in 1660. The talented apprentice boys of the Acting Companies lived in the families of the actors who trained them. John Heminges' wife had fourteen children, yet she still took in apprentices, who later remembered her with great affection.

Twelfth Night, probably first performed for the end of Christmas festivities of 1602, was popular for the scenes that show the tricking of the steward Malvolio, who is persuaded that his mistress, the Lady Olivia, is in love with him, particularly liking him in yellow stockings with cross garters. Digges recalled how 'Lo, in a trice/ The cockpit galleries, boxes, all are full,/To hear Malvolio that cross-gartered gull'. Yet the charm of the play lies in its range of moods. Love, here, is bitter-sweet. Viola, disguised as a youth, is secretly in love with her master, Count Orsino.

Viola, disguised as a youth, is secretly in love with her master Orsino, in Twelfth Night.

VIOLA   My father had a daughter loved a man
          As might be, perhaps, were I a woman,
          I should your lordship.
ORSINO   And what's her history?
VIOLA   A blank, my lord. She never told her love
          But let concealment, like a worm i'th'bud,
          Feed on her damask cheek. She pined in thought,
          And with a green and yellow melancholy
          She sat like patience on a monument,
          Smiling at grief. Was not this love indeed?

                              (*Twelfth Night*, II, iv)

Hamlet, possibly written in 1600 and revised later, has a peculiar fascination that makes it what the poet T. S. Eliot called 'The Mona Lisa of literature'. Based on an old Scandinavian folk tale by the Danish writer, Saxo Grammaticus, and on previous play versions, one perhaps by Thomas Kyd, it was an instant success: '*Hamlet*', wrote Anthony Scoloher in 1604, 'pleases all.' In what the journalist, C. E. Montague described as 'this monstrous Gothic castle of a poem, with its baffled half lights and glooms', the centre of interest lies in young Prince Hamlet, in his 'inky cloak' and suit of 'solemn black', who is distressed by his father's sudden death and disturbed by his mother's hasty re-marriage to his uncle, Claudius. The play displays astonishing moments of drama – the appearance of the ghost of Hamlet's father, the play within a play, the killing of Polonius, the tragic madness and death of Ophelia, and the final duel. However, always related to these are the broodings of Hamlet's soliloquies: on mortality and the afterlife,

The drowning of the mad Ophelia is one of the most poignant episodes in the tragedy of Hamlet. *The Victorian artist, John Millais, recreated the river scene described in Queen Gertrude's speech: 'There is a willow grows aslant a brook.'*

on revenge and action. In dialogue, too, Hamlet meditates on the fate of humanity, for example when he contemplates the skull of Yorick, the former court jester:

FIRST CLOWN This same skull, sir, was Yorick's skull, the King's jester.
HAMLET This?
FIRST CLOWN E'en that.
HAMLET Let me see.
(He takes the skull)
Alas, poor Yorick. I knew him, Horatio – a fellow of infinite jest, of most excellent fancy. He hath borne me on his back a thousand times; and now, how abhorréd my imagination is! My gorge rises at it. Here hung those lips that I have kissed I know not how oft. Where be your gibes now, your gambols, your songs, your flashes of merriment that were wont to set the table on a roar? Not one now to mock your own grinning? Quite chop fallen? Now get you to my lady's chamber and tell her let her paint an inch thick, to this favour she must come. Make her laugh at that.

(*Hamlet*, V, i)

Hamlet reflects on man's mortality as he looks at the skull of the court jester, Yorick.

The Earl of Essex, once the Queen's favourite, led an unsuccessful revolt against her in 1601. He was beheaded in the Tower.

The Earl of Essex, once the Queen's favourite, led an unsuccessful revolt against her in 1601. He was beheaded in the Tower.

Below *Queen Elizabeth in old age: Death, standing behind her, shows that her life is ending. The last years of her reign were troubled.*

The late Elizabethan years were darkened by the fall of the Earl of Essex, once the Queen's favourite. After his unsuccessful campaign in Ireland in 1599, he fell into disgrace. Frustration led him to his futile rebellion of 1601, when he and his followers planned to seize the Queen and dismiss her Ministers. When his march on the City of London failed, Essex was arrested, tried and beheaded. Shakespeare's former patron, Southampton, who supported Essex, was involved in the plot and imprisoned in the Tower. The Chamberlain's Men narrowly escaped being implicated. On the eve of the revolt, they had rashly agreed to present the history play *Richard II*, which showed the deposing of an unpopular monarch. Shakespeare's sympathies were, perhaps, with Essex. Certainly he disappointed some people by not writing an elegy for Queen Elizabeth when she died in March 1603. Henry Chettle, in 'England's Mourning Garment', noticed with surprise that Shakespeare did not:

> Drop from his honeyed muse one sable tear
> To mourn her death that graced his desert
> And to his lays opened her royal ear.

6 The Early Jacobean Years

The new king, James I of England and VI of Scotland, the first Stuart, had no sooner arrived in London than, in the re-arrangement of the Royal household, the Chamberlain's Men were appointed as the King's Men, 'freely to use and exercise the art and faculty of playing comedies, tragedies, histories, interludes . . . stage plays and such others . . . for the recreation of our loving subjects and for our solace and pleasure'. Shakespeare and his fellows were each granted $4\frac{1}{2}$ yards of scarlet cloth to make themselves liveries for the King's coronation procession. James was a generous patron: one count estimates that his players acted for him 187 times up to 1616, more than all the other London companies put together. Shakespeare's plays were most often called for, although the Clerk of the Revels's accounts regularly called him Shaxberd.

Some of the Jacobean plays seem intended to flatter James. The King's pompous views on monarchy had been set out in his book, *Basilicon Doron*. He loved to think of himself as a model of justice and mercy, so that the trial scene in *The Merchant of Venice* was a favourite of his. *Measure for Measure*, the first of Shakespeare's so-called 'problem comedies', which explores the conflicting claims of justice and mercy, may have been written to appeal to his interests.

Opposite *James I (and VI of Scotland), who succeeded Elizabeth in 1603, took a keen interest in drama and became the new patron of Shakespeare's company.*

Macbeth was most obviously written to please the King. Shakespeare telescoped various details from Holinshed's history, including the fictitious character, Banquo, whom James regarded as an ancestor, and adding the witches because he knew of James's preoccupation with witchcraft (he had written a book on the subject and had been responsible for hounding hundreds of unfortunate women to death). To show the terrible consequences of killing a king would also impress James, especially after the attempt on his life in the Gunpowder Plot, which had stunned the country in 1605. Shakespeare transforms Macbeth from a warrior king, as he appears in Holinshed, into a complex character capable of evil, for whom nonetheless we feel pity, misled as he is by the double-talk (or 'equivocation', a word much used in the Gunpowder Plot trials) of the witches. Here, upon hearing the news of his wife's suicide, Macbeth contemplates the end of a life which, as a result of a self-perpetuating chain of evil deeds, has been reduced to a nightmare of fear and despair:

The Court Revels Account noted frequent payments to the King's Men for plays performed at Court. The clerk has misspelt Shakespeare's name as 'Shaxberd'.

The tormented
Macbeth, as portrayed
by Laurence Olivier.

Tomorrow, and tomorrow, and tomorrow,
Creeps in this petty pace from day to day,
To the last syllable of recorded time;
And all our yesterdays have lighted fools
The way to dusty death. Out, out, brief candle!
Life's but a walking shadow, a poor player,
That struts and frets his hour upon the stage,
And then is heard no more; it is a tale
Told by an idiot, full of sound and fury,
Signifying nothing.

(*Macbeth*, V, v)

The early Jacobean years were the high point of Shakespeare's achievement. *Othello* was performed before James at Whitehall in 1604. Here, obsessive jealousy, the 'green-eyed monster', stirred in him by the evil Iago, leads Othello to strangle his wife, Desdemona, because he suspects she has been unfaithful to him.

(*Enter Othello with a light. He draws back a curtain, revealing Desdemona asleep in her bed.*)

Othello's obsessive jealousy compels him to strangle his wife, Desdemona.

OTHELLO ... Put out the light, and then put out the light.
If I quench thee, thou flaming minister,
I can again thy former light restore
Should I repent me; but once put out thy light,
Thou cunning'st pattern of excellent nature,
I know not where is that Promethean heat
That can thy light relume. When I have plucked thy
     rose
I cannot give it vital growth again.
It needs must wither ...

(*Othello*, V, ii)

The exotic Egyptian Queen, Cleopatra, who fascinates the Roman leader, Antony.

Antony and Cleopatra, which the poet Coleridge called 'this astonishing drama ... by far the most wonderful of all Shakespeare's historical plays', continues the story of the consequences of Julius Caesar's death. The language of this story of tragic, obsessive, consuming passion magnificently displays the style of the mature Shakespeare. His source, North's Plutarch, was rich and colourful, as in the picture of Queen Cleopatra of Egypt in her barge:

> ... the poop whereof was of gold, the sails of purple, and the oars of silver, which kept stroke in rowing after the sound of flutes, hautboys, cithern, viols ... She was laid under a pavilion of cloth of gold of tissue ...
>
> (Thomas North, *Lives of the noble Grecians and Romans*, 1579)

yet Shakespeare turns this rich picture into something even more exotic, more sumptuous:

> The barge she sat in, like a burnished throne
> Burned on the water. The poop was beaten gold;
> Purple the sails, and so perfumed that
> The winds were love-sick with them. The oars were silver
> Which to the tune of flutes kept stroke, and made
> The water which they beat to follow faster,
> As amorous of their strokes. For her own person
> It beggared all description. She did lie
> In her pavilion – cloth of gold, of tissue –

81

O'erpicturing that Venus where we see
The fancy outwork nature . . .

(Antony and Cleopatra, II, ii)

Whereas in his early work Shakespeare used long, elaborate comparisons, now he skips impressionistically from idea to idea. In this speech, for example, where Antony compares his failure with Octavius Caesar's success, Shakespeare moves swiftly from dogs to sweets to trees; nor is he afraid to invent a new verb: to 'spaniel'.

All come to this? The hearts
That spanieled me at heels, to whom I gave
Their wishes, do discandy, melt their sweets
On blossoming Caesar; and this pine is barked
That overtopped them all.

(Antony and Cleopatra, IV, xii)

In *King Lear*, Shakespeare reached his height as an artist. The agony of Lear in his madness in the storm, the stunning conclusion, where Lear enters with the dead Cordelia in his arms, has proved too much for some audiences. Dr Johnson claimed, 'I was many years so shocked by Cordelia's death that I know not whether I ever endured to read again the last scenes of the play till I undertook to revise them again as an editor.' Eighteenth-century audiences agreed with him, and a version of the play by Nahum Tate, which gave it a happy ending ('Old Lear shall be a king again') was played on stages from 1681 to early Victorian times. Lear's last speeches have a terrible simplicity.

Howl, howl, howl, howl! O, you are men of stones:
Had I your tongues and eyes, I'd use them so
That heaven's vault should crack. She's gone for ever!
I know when one is dead and when one lives.
She's dead as earth. Lend me a looking-glass.
If that her breath will mist or stain the stone
Why then she lives . . .
        . . .No, no, no life?
Why should a dog, a horse, a rat have life,
And thou no breath at all? Thou'lt come no more.
Never, never, never, never, never.

(King Lear, V, iii)

Shakespeare's fame was now such that even plays that he did not write – *Locrine, The London Prodigal, A Yorkshire Tragedy* – were put out under his name. Success did not destroy his personal charm, however. Surviving tributes see him as 'friendly'; 'generous ye are in mind and mood'; 'so dear loved a neighbour'. Jonson's adjective 'gentle' seems best to sum him up. Early biographers echo this: John Aubrey heard he was 'a handsome, well-shaped man; very good company, and of a very ready and pleasant smooth wit', while Nicholas Rowe heard of him as 'a good natured man, of great sweetness in his manners and a most agreeable companion'. An anecdote about the well-known Mermaid tavern in London's Bread Street, said to have been a writers' meeting-place, gives us a glimpse, sadly not a trustworthy one, of the poet with his friend, Ben Jonson.

King Lear and his daughter Cordelia, painted by William Blake. For a hundred years, the end of King Lear *was thought too painful to play on the stage.*

Many were the wit-combats betwixt him and Ben Jonson,
which two I beheld like a Spanish great galleon, and
an English man-of-war; Master Jonson (like the former)
was built far higher in learning; solid, but slow in his
performances. Shakespeare, with the English man-of-
war, lesser in bulk, but lighter in sailing, could turn with
all tides, tack about and take advantage of all winds,
by the quickness of his wit and invention . . .

(Thomas Fuller, *History of the
worthies of England*, 1662)

In 1608, the King's Men took over the Blackfriars
Theatre, within the City walls. James Burbage had refur-
bished this former dining hall in 1597, but local people
had objected successfully against its use for showing
plays. Since then, it had been used by the troupe of
boy actors which were a temporary theatre craze in 1600,
and which Hamlet protested against as 'little eyases'

(hawks). The Blackfriars was small, seating 700 people, as compared to the 3,000 at the Globe. Entry prices were higher, the audience wealthier and more sophisticated. The new theatre eventually proved more profitable than the Globe, where the King's Men still played in summer. It had an intimate atmosphere, well suited to present the subtleties of the exquisite late tragi-comedies: *Cymbeline*, *The Winter's Tale* and *The Tempest*.

> Fear no more the heat o'th'sun,
> Nor the furious winter's rages.
> Thou thy worldly task has done,
> Home art gone and ta'en thy wages.
> Golden lads and girls all must
> As chimney-sweepers, come to dust.
>
> (*Cymbeline*, IV, ii)

The Tempest (1610–11), is a supernatural story of a desert island, perhaps based on a real shipwreck in the Bermudas at this time. Prospero, the magician who lives on the island with his daughter Miranda, his attendant spirit Aerial, and the monster Caliban, conjures up a wedding masque to celebrate his daughter's marriage

At the end of The Tempest, *Prospero the magician promises to abandon his book of spells and magic staff. Some have seen in this gesture a picture of Shakespeare's own farewell to his work for the stage. Yet he was active in London theatre until at least 1613.*

to Ferdinand, a shipwrecked Prince. At the play's conclusion, Prospero compares acting to human existence itself:

> Our revels now are ended. These our actors,
> As I foretold you, were all spirits, and
> Are melted into air, into thin air;
> And like the baseless fabric of this vision,
> The cloud-capped towers, the gorgeous palaces,
> The solemn temples, the great globe itself,
> Yea, all which it inherit, shall dissolve;
> And, like this insubstantial pageant faded,
> Leave not a wrack behind. We are such stuff
> As dreams are made on, and our little life
> Is rounded with a sleep . . .

> (*The Tempest*, IV, i)

When Prospero announces that he will give up his magic ('I'll break my staff . . . and deeper than did ever plummet sound, I'll drown my book'), some people have felt that this is Shakespeare himself, renouncing his magic talent for writing before his retirement. This is fanciful. He was still active in London after 1611, even buying a new house there, near Blackfriars, in 1613. The winter of 1612–13 was especially busy, with its festivities to mark the Royal Wedding of James's daughter, Elizabeth, to a German prince. No fewer than 14 plays were performed by the King's Men during February alone. Nor was *The Tempest* his last play. He combined with a rising star of the Jacobean theatre, John Fletcher, to write *The Two Noble Kinsmen*, based on Chaucer's 'Knight's Tale', and *Cardenio*, a play that has been lost, although it was recorded at a Court performance in 1613. *Henry VIII*, or *All is true*, was another collaboration with Fletcher.

During the winter of 1612–13, the King's Men acted many times as part of the celebrations marking the marriage of King James's daughter to a German prince.

It was during a performance of this play at the Globe, in June 1613, that a stage cannon fired a burning paper ball on to the thatched roof of the theatre, which was soon completely destroyed by fire. An eye-witness, Sir Henry Wotton, described the disaster in a letter:

> Now King Henry making a masque at the Cardinal Wolsey's house, and certain chambers [guns] being shot off at his entry, some of the paper, or other stuff, wherewith one of them was stopped, did light on the thatch, where ... their eyes more attentive to the show, it kindled inwardly, and ran round like a train [fuse], consuming within less than an hour the whole house to the very grounds.
>
> This was the fatal period of that virtuous fabric, wherein yet nothing did perish but wood and straw, and a few forsaken cloaks; only one man had his breeches set on fire, that would perhaps have broiled him, if he had not put it out with bottled ale ...

(Sir Henry Wotton,
letter, 2 July 1613)

Cattermole imagined Shakespeare enjoying retirement in the garden of New Place. The famous mulberry tree that he planted stands behind the table.

A new and more splendid building, with a tiled roof, was soon erected on the site, the expense falling on the sharers. Perhaps it was the burning of the Globe that decided Shakespeare to sell his share in the theatre and remove to Stratford for the rest of his life, there to enjoy, as Nicholas Rowe imagined, 'ease, retirement and the conversation of his friends.'

7 The Last Years

In Stratford, there were family preoccupations. Shakespeare's elder daughter, Susanna ('Witty above her sex . . . something of Shakespeare was in that', says her epitaph) had married a doctor, John Hall, in 1607. He had a fine local reputation for his craft, no matter how crude the remedies listed in his case-book, 'Select Observations', now seem. The couple supposedly lived at a large, pleasant house, now known as Hall's Croft, by the church. In February, 1616, Judith married a much less reliable husband, Thomas Quiney, a wine-shop keeper, whose family had long been friendly rivals of the Shakespeares.

There were business preoccupations, too. Shakespeare busied himself with buying and selling, and the petty law suits that fascinated so many people of his time. He had added steadily to his estate by purchasing farmland or tithes (the right to receive farm taxes). His tithe income was threatened by an unsuccessful attempt by a local landowner to enclose (hedge and cultivate) common land at Welcombe. Luckily his town houses were not touched by the disastrous fire of 1614, which destroyed 54 Stratford buildings.

Shakespeare made his will in 1616, revising it in March, after his daughter's wedding. Although he describes himself as 'in perfect health and memory', he was probably already fatally ill. His signatures, say experts, show signs of 'weakness and malformation'. The will is interesting for the details it gives of his estate and because it names the people he cared for most. The Halls were left most of the goods and property, including New Place. Judith received substantial money and 'my broad silver-gilt bowl'. To his sister, Joan, went 'all my wearing apparel' and the right to live in the Henley Street house. The celebrated bequest to his wife, Anne – 'Item: I give unto my wife my second best bed' – seems insulting but is used as a conventional phrase in other wills: it seems that this was the marriage bed, with its sentimental associations, the best bed being usually reserved for guests. In any case Anne would have been well provided for, receiving a third of the estate under English common law. Besides his family, he remembered old comrades from the King's Men, John Heminges, Richard Burbage and Henry Condell, leaving them money to buy memorial rings.

The will is Shakespeare's attempt to pass on his carefully gathered wealth. However, the hoped-for grandsons mentioned in the will were not born to Susanna, or did not survive in Judith's family. When his grand-

A page from Shakespeare's will of 1616, showing his handwriting 'By me' and the signature, which, say experts, shows signs of illness and physical decline. The witnesses have signed on the left.

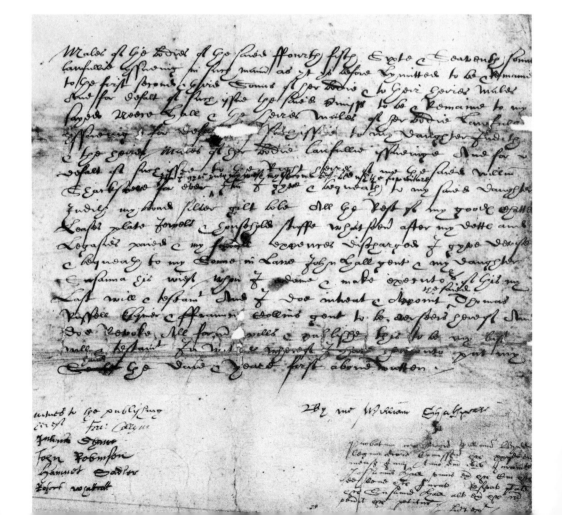

daughter, Elizabeth, died in 1670, the direct family line ended and the land, houses and goods that he so cherished were disposed of to strangers. His true estate was his set of plays, the real investment of his energy and powers, that was, as Ben Jonson could see,

> so rammed with life
> That it shall gather strength of life with being,
> And live hereafter, more admired than now.

The last glimpse of the writer is given in a hearsay note by the Stratford vicar who interviewed Judith:

> Shakespeare, Drayton and Ben Jonson had a merry meeting, and it seems, drank too hard, for Shakespeare died of a fever there contracted.
>
> (John Ward, *Diary*, 1661–3)

Dr Hall's notes on patients begin only in 1617, so we do not have an exact record of his father-in-law's last illness. Shakespeare died, aged 52, on his birthday, 23 April 1616, and was buried two days later in Holy Trinity Church. His grave was said to be 17 feet deep. On the slab that covers it is a crude warning verse, written perhaps by the poet himself.

> Good friend, for Jesus' sake forbear
> To dig the dust enclosed here;
> Blessed be the man that spares these stones
> And cursed be he that moves my bones.
>
> (Gravestone epitaph)

Shakespeare's grave in Stratford Church with its epitaph warning against its disturbance.

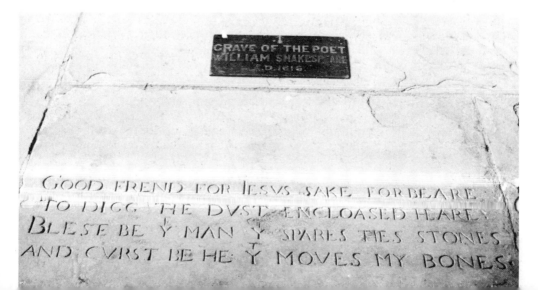

Stratford sextons, anxious to find new burial space inside the church, did sometimes open graves and remove remains to the nearby charnel house. One anecdote claims that Shakespeare had a horror of that place, and wrote his gravediggers' scene in *Hamlet* after seeing its 'rattling bones ... reeky shanks and yellow chapless skulls'.

The monument, with its painted bust, carved by Geerart Janssen at his stone-mason's shop near the Globe in London, soon attracted pilgrims. Yet the real memorial was the First Folio collection of his plays, which was soon being prepared by his actor colleagues. His friend, Leonard Digges, was quick to see the relative value of bust and book:

> When that stone is rent
> And time dissolves thy Stratford monument,
> Here we alive shall view thee still. This book
> When brass and marble fade, shall make thee look
> Fresh to all ages.

> (Leonard Digges, First Folio, 1623)

After his death, two survivors of the old Chamberlain's Men, John Heminges and Henry Condell, both known for their kindness, decided to keep Shakespeare's memory alive by collecting and publishing his plays in a grand Folio-sized edition. Books came in two sizes: Folio, where a full sheet of paper was folded once to give two large pages, and Quarto, where it was folded twice, producing four smaller pages. The editors were being deliberately ambitious: most plays were put out as Quartos, only Ben Jonson having dared to produce a Folio collection of his own writing. However, they stated their aim:

> We have but collected them, and done an office to the dead to procure his orphans [his plays] guardians, without ambition either of self profit or fame, only to keep the memory of so worthy a friend and fellow alive as was our Shakespeare.

> (Heminges and Condell, preface
> to First Folio, 1623)

Mr. WILLIAM

SHAKESPEARES

COMEDIES,
HISTORIES, &
TRAGEDIES.

Published according to the True Originall Copies.

Martin Droeshout sculpsit London.

LONDON
Printed by Isaac Iaggard, and Ed. Blount. 1623.

*Hamlet's soliloquy 'To be or not to be': the confusions of the 'bad' Quarto text (**right**), perhaps taken down from an actor's memories, contrast with the First Folio text (**opposite**).*

Ham. To be, or not to be, I there's the point,
To Die, to sleepe, is that all? I all:
No, to sleepe, to dreame, I mary there it goes,
For in that dreame of death, when wee awake,
And borne before an euerlasting Iudge,
From whence no passenger euer retur'nd,
The vndiscouered country, at whose sight
The happy smile, and the accursed damn'd.
But for this, the ioyfull hope of this,
Whol'd beare the scornes and flattery of the world,
Scorned by the right rich, the rich curssed of the poore?
The widow being opprested, the orphan wrong'd,
The taste of hunger, or a tirants raigne,
And thousand more calamities besides,
To grunt and sweate vnder this weary life,
When that he may his full *Quietus* make,
With a bare bodkin, who would this indure,
But for a hope of something after death?
Which pusles the braine, and doth confound the sence,
Which makes vs rather beare those euilles we haue,
Than flie to others that we know not of.
I that, O this conscience makes cowardes of vs all,
Lady in thy orizons, be all my sinnes remembred.

They sensibly advised their audience to 'Read him therefore, and again, and again'.

Working from the precious manuscripts, which the King's Men still held, and a few of the 'good' (that is, accurate) Quarto texts published in Shakespeare's lifetime, the two editors brought together 36 plays, 18 of them never before printed. They resented the 'bad' Quartos, put out without the author's permission: 'stolen and surreptitious copies, maimed and deformed by the frauds and stealths of injurious imposters ...' However, their own Folio was so carelessly printed that it was full of mistakes, and a modern editor still has to use the Quartos, good and bad, in preparing a new edition.

Enter Hamlet.

Ham. To be, or not to be, that is the Queſtion:
Whether 'tis Nobler in the minde to ſuffer
The Slings and Arrowes of outragious Fortune,
Or to take Armes againſt a Sea of troubles,
And by oppoſing end them : to dye, to ſleepe
No more ; and by a ſleepe, to ſay we end
The Heart-ake, and the thouſand Naturall ſhockes
That Fleſh is heyre too ? 'Tis a conſummation
Deuoutly to be wiſh'd. To dye to ſleepe,
To ſleepe, perchance to Dreame ; I, there's the rub,
For in that ſleepe of death, what dreames may come,
When we haue ſhuffiel'd off this mortall coile,
Muſt giue vs pawſe. There's the reſpect
That makes Calamity of ſo long life :
For who would beare the Whips and Scornes of time,
The Oppreſſors wrong, the poore mans Contumely,
The pangs of diſpriz'd Loue, the Lawes delay,
The inſolence of Office, and the Spurnes
That patient merit of the vnworthy takes,
When he himſelfe might his *Quietus* make
With a bare Bodkin ? Who would theſe Fardles beare
To grunt and ſweat vnder a weary life,
But that the dread of ſomething after death,
The vndiſcouered Countrey, from whoſe Borne
No Traueller returnes, Puzels the will,
And makes vs rather beare thoſe illes we haue,
Then flye to others that we know not of.
Thus Conſcience does make Cowards of vs all,
And thus the Natiue hew of Reſolution
Is ſicklied o're, with the pale caſt of Thought,
And enterprizes of great pith and moment,
With this regard their Currants turne away,
And looſe the name of Action. Soft you now,
The faire *Ophelia?* Nimph, in thy Orizons
Be all my ſinnes remembred.

To introduce the book there were verse tributes, the
best of which was by Ben Jonson, who addressed Shakespeare as 'Soul of the Age! The applause, delight, the
wonder of our stage!'

> Sweet swan of Avon! what a sight it were
>   To see thee in our waters yet appear,
> And make those flights upon the banks of Thames
>   That did so take Eliza and our James!
> But stay, I see thee in the hemisphere
>   Advanced, and made a constellation there!
> Shine forth, thou star of poets . . .

(Ben Jonson, memorial poem to
Shakespeare, 1623)

Opposite *The
passion for
Shakespeare begun in
the eighteenth century
culminated in the
foundation of the
Memorial Theatre in
Stratford in 1879.*

Succeeding centuries have judged Shakespeare according to the ebb and flow of social, theatrical and literary fashions. To the neo-classicists (those who wished art to be governed by rules established by ancient Greek and Roman critics) of the late seventeenth and early eighteenth centuries, Shakespeare was talented but crude, and sometimes offensive. Accordingly his plays were cut and rewritten, when they were performed at all. The mighty critic, Samuel Johnson, did much to restore the playwright's reputation in his edition of 1765: 'Shakespeare opens a mine which contains gold and diamonds in unexhaustible plenty'. Johnson's friend, David Garrick, the actor, recreated the great roles on stage, and established the Shakespeare cult with his Stratford Festival in 1769. To Romantic critics of the early nineteenth century, 'myriad-minded' Shakespeare was a god-like being. In his works, wrote William Hazlitt, you see 'a mind reflecting ages of past and present . . . all the people that ever lived are there.' Victorian biographers saw Shakespeare as the human type their era admired: the self-made man who got on. The rising chorus of patriotic and imperial pride claimed him as a precious part of the nation's heritage. 'He is the grandest thing we have done' wrote Thomas Carlyle in *On Heroes* (1840). 'The Indian Empire will go some day but this Shakespeare . . . lasts forever with us.'

Debates surrounding Shakespeare's works are very much alive today: almost anything one group of critics says about them will be disputed by another. The ideas of A. C. Bradley, writing in 1905, and E. M. W. Tillyard's works written in the 1940s have been taught in schools ever since; yet they were challenged by Wilbur Sanders and many others during the 1960s, and are now hotly disputed by critics such as Jonathan Dollimore and Alan Sinfield, whose approach to Shakespeare and his historical context is radically different. Today, feminist critics are opening up new critical debates by discussing the role played by women in Shakespeare's work (see the further reading list).

The huge Shakespeare scholarship industry of the twentieth century, based on universities across the world, allows us to fully appreciate the power of Shakespeare's words and the strength of his stagecraft. Film and television now preserve great performances, and

Shakespeare
MEMORIAL THEATRE,
STRATFORD-ON-AVON.

INAUGURAL FESTIVAL
on
SHAKESPEARE'S BIRTHDAY, WEDNESDAY, APRIL 23, 1879,
AND FOLLOWING DAYS.

WEDNESDAY EVENING, APRIL 23rd,

MUCH ADO ABOUT NOTHING

On this occasion, the Council have the honour to announce that Mrs. THEODORE MARTIN (HELEN FAUCIT) has most kindly consented to appear.

Benedick	Mr. BARRY SULLIVAN
Don Pedro	Mr. LUIGI LABLACHE
Don John	Mr. HERBERT JENNER
Claudio	Mr. EDWARD COMPTON
Leonato	Mr. RYDER
Balthazar	Mr. W. H. CUMMINGS

Who will Sing, "Sigh no more, Ladies."

Dogberry	Mr. W. H. STEPHENS
Verges	Mr. FRANK BARSBY
Beatrice	Mrs. THEODORE MARTIN (HELEN FAUCIT)
Hero	Miss WALLIS
Ursula	Miss HUDSPETH
Margaret	Miss GOLIEN

Previous to the Performance, A DEDICATORY ADDRESS, written by Dr. WESTLAND MARSTON, will be recited by Miss KATE FIELD.

THURSDAY EVENING, APRIL 24th,

HAMLET

Hamlet	Mr. BARRY SULLIVAN
Claudius	Mr. HERBERT JENNER
Polonius	Mr. W. H. STEPHENS
Laertes	Mr. EDWARD COMPTON
Horatio	Mr. LUIGI LABLACHE
Ghost	Mr. RYDER
First Gravedigger	Mr. FRANK BARSBY
Gertrude	Mrs. CHARLES CALVERT
Ophelia	Miss WALLIS
Actress	Miss EMMERSON

FRIDAY EVENING, APRIL 25th,

A CONCERT

The Music of which is associated with the Works of Shakespeare.

Madame ARABELLA GODDARD, Mrs. OSGOOD, Miss KATE FIELD, Madame ANTOINETTE STERLING, Mr. W. SHAKESPEARE, Mr. W. H. CUMMINGS, and Mr. SANTLEY. The LONDON CONCERT GLEE UNION, under the direction of Mr. FRED WALKER.

Conductor ... SIR JULIUS BENEDICT.

SATURDAY AFTERNOON, APRIL 26th,

HAMLET

Will be repeated.

Hamlet	Mr. BARRY SULLIVAN
Claudius	Mr. HERBERT JENNER
Polonius	Mr. W. H. STEPHENS
Laertes	Mr. EDWARD COMPTON
Horatio	Mr. LUIGI LABLACHE
Ghost	Mr. RYDER
First Gravedigger	Mr. FRANK BARSBY
Gertrude	Mrs. CHARLES CALVERT
Ophelia	Miss WALLIS
Actress	Miss EMMERSON

MONDAY AFTERNOON, APRIL 28th,
Mr. SAMUEL BRANDRAM will Recite

"THE TEMPEST."

The Songs incidental to the Play will be sung by Miss de FONBLANQUE.

On MONDAY EVENING, APRIL 28th, and THURSDAY EVENING, MAY 1st,

MUCH ADO ABOUT NOTHING

Benedick	Mr. BARRY SULLIVAN
Don Pedro	Mr. LUIGI LABLACHE
Don John	Mr. HERBERT JENNER
Claudio	Mr. EDWARD COMPTON
Leonato	Mr. RYDER
Balthazar	Mr. W. H. CUMMINGS

Who will Sing, "Sigh no more, Ladies."

Dogberry	Mr. W. H. STEPHENS
Verges	Mr. FRANK BARSBY
Beatrice	Miss WALLIS
Hero	Miss EMMERSON
Ursula	Miss HUDSPETH
Margaret	Miss GOLIEN

On TUESDAY EVENING, APRIL 29th, and FRIDAY EVENING, MAY 2nd,

HAMLET

Hamlet	Mr. BARRY SULLIVAN
Claudius	Mr. HERBERT JENNER
Polonius	Mr. W. H. STEPHENS
Laertes	Mr. EDWARD COMPTON
Horatio	Mr. LUIGI LABLACHE
Ghost	Mr. RYDER
First Gravedigger	Mr. FRANK BARSBY
Gertrude	Mrs. CHARLES CALVERT
Ophelia	Miss WALLIS
Actress	Miss EMMERSON

On WEDNESDAY EVENING APRIL 30th, and SATURDAY AFTERNOON, MAY 3rd,

AS YOU LIKE IT

Jaques	Mr. BARRY SULLIVAN
Duke	Mr. ALLERTON
Banished Duke	Mr. LUIGI LABLACHE
Orlando	Mr. EDWARD COMPTON
Adam	Mr. RYDER
Touchstone	Mr. FRANK BARSBY
Amiens	Mr. W. H. CUMMINGS

Who will Sing, "Blow, blow, thou Wintry Wind."

Rosalind	Miss WALLIS
Audry	Miss HUDSPETH
Celia	Miss EMMERSON
Phœbe	Miss GOLIEN

Return Tickets at Reduced Fares.—SPECIAL TRAINS after the Performances to Leamington Every Evening; to Birmingham on 23rd and 24th; and to Worcester on 25th and 28th, stopping at intermediate stations.

For further particulars see Official Programmes, to be had Price 6d. on application to the Festival Ticket Office, New Place, Stratford-on-Avon.

All the Evening Performances will begin at 7 o'clock; doors open at 6·15 p.m. Those in the Afternoon begin at 3 o'clock; doors open at 2·15 p.m.

PRICES OF ADMISSION (for Seats Numbered and Reserved)—

WEDNESDAY, April 23rd, 20s., 10s., & 5s. THURSDAY, April 24th, 20s., 10s., 5s., & 2s.6d. REMAINDER OF FESTIVAL, 10s., 5s., & 2s.6d.

give Shakespeare a vast international audience. One theme of *Shakespeare, our contemporary* (1964), an important critical book by the Polish writer, Jan Kott, is that Shakespeare never goes out of date: each generation and each society finds its own preoccupations reflected in his work. Ben Jonson said the same thing three and a half centuries ago in his memorial poem:

He was not of an age, but for all time.

Glossary

Blank verse Unrhymed verse. Each line has the same metrical form, known as iambic pentameter: five poetic 'feet', each containing one unstressed and one stressed syllable.

Oñce móre | ŭntó | thĕ bréach | dĕar friénds | oñce móre
Or close the wall up with our English dead.

Shakespeare made blank verse into an astonishingly flexible and subtle medium.

Classical Connected with the literature of Ancient Greece and Rome.

Collaboration Work prepared jointly by several writers.

Elegy Poem of mourning.

Genre A type of literature (i.e. play, poem, essay etc.)

Groundlings Those who paid one penny to stand in the theatre arena to watch the play.

Jacobean Concerned with the reign of James I (Latin: Jacobus=James).

Manuscript Book or document written by hand.

Masque Spectacular musical entertainment popular at the court of James I.

Morality play Medieval/early Tudor play usually offering a religious message.

Narrative poem One that tells a story.

Parody Imitation (usually mocking) of an author or a style.

Properties Moveable articles used on stage during a play.

Prose Ordinary non-metrical language. Shakespeare was a master of prose as well as verse (see speeches of Falstaff and Shylock).

Pun Word used humorously to suggest two different meanings.

Revels Christmas season entertainments at Court.

Rhetoric The art of persuasive speaking and writing.

Secular Non-religious.

Sharer Senior member of acting company, who shared the expenses and the profits of play performances. Unusually, the Chamberlain's Men owned not only scripts, costumes and properties, but also the Globe Theatre.

Sonnet Fourteen line poem of set verse form, devised by the Italian poet Petrarch and much imitated in England in the 1590s. The Shakespearean sonnet has three quatrains (groups of four alternately rhymed lines) and a couplet (two rhymed lines).

ABAB CDCD EFEF GG

Each line has a pentameter rhythm, like that of blank verse.

Thăt tíme | ŏf yéar | thŏu máyst | iň mé | bĕhóld |.

Tetralogy Series of four plays in a sequence.
Trilogy Series of three plays in a sequence.

List of Dates

(Dates for composition of plays and poems, variant titles and collaborating authors are based on points suggested in *William Shakespeare: the Complete Works* ed. S. Wells and G. Taylor, Oxford 1986)

Life

1564	23 April? Birth at Stratford.
1568	Father made High Bailiff (Mayor) of Stratford.
1576	James Burbage opened the Theatre in London.
1582	December? Marriage to Anne Hathaway.
1583	Birth of daughter, Susanna.
1585	Birth of twins, Hamnet and Judith.
1585–92	The 'lost years'.
1587	Move to London?
	Marlowe writes *Tamburlaine*.
1588	Defeat of Spanish Armada.
1592	Robert Greene's attack on the 'upstart crow'.
	Plague closes theatres.
1593	Death of Christopher Marlowe.
1595	Mentioned as playing before Elizabeth I with the Chamberlain's men.
1597	Bought New Place, Stratford.
1598	Praised by Francis Meres.
1599	Opening of Globe Theatre.
1601	Rebellion and execution of Essex.
	Death of John Shakespeare.
1603	Death of Elizabeth I.
	Accession of James I.
	Chamberlain's Men became the King's Men.
1605	The gunpowder plot.
1607	Susanna's marriage to Dr John Hall.
1608	Birth of granddaughter, Elizabeth.
1612	Mentioned as witness in Montjoy-Beloff case in London.
1613	Globe Theatre destroyed by fire.
	Retirement to Stratford?

1616   Makes and revises will.
            April 23: Death, aged 52.
            Buried in Holy Trinity Church, Stratford.

Works

1589?	*Two Gentlemen of Verona*
1590	*Titus Andronicus*
1590–1	*Henry VI pt. 2* (The first part of the contention)
1591	*Henry VI pt. 3* (Richard, Duke of York)
1591?	*The Taming of the Shrew*
1592	*Henry VI pt. 1* (with other authors)
1592–3	*Richard III*
1593	*Venus and Adonis* (poem)
1593–4	*Love's Labours Lost*
1594	*Love's Labours Won?* (lost play)
	The Rape of Lucrece (poem)
	The Comedy of Errors

The eighteenth-century artist, William Blake, brought the Droeshout engraving to life in his painting of Shakespeare.

1594–5	*A Midsummer Night's Dream*
	Romeo and Juliet
	Sonnets?
1595	*Richard II*
1595–6	*King John*
1596–7	*The Merchant of Venice*
	Henry IV Parts 1 and 2
1597	*Merry Wives of Windsor*
1598–9	*Much Ado about Nothing*
1599	*Henry V*
	Julius Caesar
1600	*As You Like It*
	Hamlet (revised later)
1601	*Twelfth Night*
1601–3	*Troilus and Cressida*
1603–4	*Othello* (revised later)
1604	*Measure for Measure*
	All's Well that ends Well
	Timon of Athens (with Thomas Middleton)
1606	*Macbeth*
	Antony and Cleopatra
1608	*King Lear* (revised 1610–11?)
	Pericles, Prince of Tyre (with George Wilkins)
	Coriolanus
1609	*Sonnets* published
1609–10	*The Winter's Tale*
1610–11	*Cymbeline*
	The Tempest
1612–13	*Cardenio* (with John Fletcher: a lost play)
1613	*All is True* (Henry VIII) (with John Fletcher)
	The Two Noble Kinsmen (with John Fletcher)
1623	First Folio Edition of the plays edited by Heminges and Condell.

Further reading

The works

WELLS, S. and TAYLOR, G. *Complete Works* (Oxford, 1986)
Individual plays and poems: New Penguin edition or New Arden edition (Methuen)

The life

CHUTE, M. *Shakespeare of London* (Souvenir Press, 1977)
SCHOENBAUM, S. *William Shakespeare: A Compact Documentary Life* (Oxford, 1977 & 1987)

Guides

CLARK, S. *A Shakespeare Dictionary* (Hutchinson, 1986)
GOODWIN, J. *A Short Guide to Shakespeare's Plays* (Heinemann, 1975)
LITTLE, R., REDSELL, P. and WILCOX, E. *The Shakespeare File* (Heinemann, 1987)

Background

BRIGGS, J. *This Stage-Play World* (Oxford University Press, 1983)
RUSSELL BROWN J. *Shakespeare and His Theatre* (Kestrel, 1982)
ROWSE, A. L. *In Shakespeare's Land* (Weidenfeld, 1986)

Critical debates

BRADLEY, A. C. *Shakespearean Tragedy* (Macmillan, 1905)
DOLLIMORE, J. *Radical Tragedy* (Harvester, 1984, University of Chicago Press, 1984)
DOLLIMORE, J. and SINFIELD, A. (eds) *Political Shakespeare* (Manchester University Press, 1985, Dover New Hampshire, 1985)
DUSINBERRE, J. *Shakespeare and the Nature of Women* (Macmillan, 1975)

GREENE, G. (ed) The Woman's Part: Feminist Criticism of Shakespeare (Illinois University Press, 1980)

SANDERS, W. *The Dramatist and The Received Idea* (Cambridge University Press, 1968)

TILLYARD, E. M. W. *The Elizabethan World Picture* 1943 (Pelican, 1986)

TILLYARD, E. M. W. *Shakespeare's History Plays* 1944 (Pelican, 1986)

Further information

Video material

Shakespeare (Famous Authors Series) Macmillan/Nelson Filmscan.

Many BBC productions of the plays are available on video from BBC Enterprises.

Classic film versions are available from Oxford Vision Research, Step Centre, Osney Mead, Oxford.

Places to visit

In Stratford-upon-Avon:
  The birthplace, Henley Street (The Shakespeare Centre)
  Nash House and New Place Gardens
  Hall's Croft
  The Grammar School (old schoolroom)
  Ann Hathaway's Cottage
  Holy Trinity Church (grave and memorial)
  Royal Shakespeare Theatre (RSC Gallery: painting and stage history)

In London:
  Shakespeare Globe Museum (part of International Globe Centre, Southwark
  Barbican and National Theatres
  The Theatre Museum, Covent Garden

Index

Numbers in **bold** refer to illustrations

Picture acknowledgments

The author and publishers would like to thank the following for allowing their illustrations to be reproduced in this book: Sarah Ainslie 45; Aldus Archive 19, 23, 50; By permission of the British Library 12, 52, 94–5; College of Arms (MS Vincent 157 no 23) 64; Donald Cooper (Photostage) 49, 61, 70–71, 72, 80, 81, 86; Dulwich College Library 48; Mary Evans Picture Library 13, 25, 29, 30, 31, 32, 33, 46, 56; Fotomas Index 15, 20, 28, 65, 93; Illustrated London News Picture Library 68; Manchester City Art Galleries 103; The Mansell Collection 26–7, 28, 39, 55; Angus McBean 79; National Film Archive 59, 69, 74; Public Record Office 78, 90; The Shakespeare Centre 8, 15, 17, 18, 24, 36, 80, 88, 91, 97, 98; Tate Gallery 58, 73, 83; Wayland Picture Library 7, 10, 16, 18, 32, 33, 34, 35, 37, 38, 40, 42, 43, 47, 54, 61, 66, 75, 77, 84, 85, 87.

We would also like to thank Oxford University Press for allowing us to reproduce one stanza from the poem 'Shall I die?' on p. 13, from *The Complete Works of William Shakespeare* edited by Stanley Wells and Gary Taylor (Oxford University Press, 1986).